The

Practicing

Mind

Bringing Discipline and Focus
Into Your Life

About the Author

For most of his life, Thomas M. Sterner has been captivated by the subject and experience of learning self-discipline. Through his life's activities, he has continuously placed himself in a position to both develop and clarify his understanding of what it means to possess this much-sought-after virtue, and to experience the reward of inner peace that accompanies its mastery.

For over 25 years, Thomas M. Sterner served as the chief concert piano technician for a major performing arts center. Throughout that time, he prepared and maintained the concert grand piano for hundreds of world-renowned musicians and symphony conductors under the most demanding circumstances. A typical workday would require his constant interaction with highly disciplined and focused artists.

As an adjunct, he operated a piano remanufacturing facility, completely rebuilding vintage grand pianos back to factory-new condition. Working on an instrument that has 88 notes is repetitious and tedious by nature, and his days were spent performing delicate procedures often hundreds of times per task with little or no room for costly errors. Being disciplined and focused was both his joy and his key to survival.

Raised in a traditional Western religion and environment, Mr. Sterner has also continued to pursue a passion for studying both Eastern thought and modern sports psychology. In his spare time, he is an accomplished musician, a private pilot, a student of archery and a long time avid golfer. His participation in and joyful experience of all of these pursuits are not only possible through his practice and application of discipline and focus, but also have placed him in a unique position in which to be able to relate to these concepts and communicate them to others.

The ability to quiet one's mind and to be able to focus one's energy at will on any particular task provides timeless, true self-empowerment by anyone's standard, but it is also the key to beginning to unlock the experience of inner peace we all find so evasive in our lives today. All of this information and experience has come together in this book, which Mr. Sterner has aptly titled "The Practicing Mind".

The
Practicing
Mind

Bringing Discipline and Focus
Into Your Life

Thomas M. Sterner

Mountain Sage Publishing
Wilmington, Delaware

Published by Mountain Sage Publishing
Wilmington, Delaware
www.mountainsagepublishing.com
Please Visit Us At www.thepracticingmind.com

Printed in the United States of America

Cover design by Cynthia A. Webb

ISBN 978-0-9776572-0-9

First Printing: March 2006
Second Printing: March 2008

Mountain Sage Publishing
products to quiet the mind

This book is dedicated to the
gentle spirit of my mother
Margaret Sterner
You taught so many, so much
with so few words

Acknowledgments

I would like to thank the people who made this book possible.

To my wife Jamie and my two daughters Margie and Melissa, I say thank you for believing in me and being patient with the long process of getting here.

To my father I must say thank you for a lifetime of support and friendship beyond any words.

Finally, to my close friend and editor (perhaps an unusual combination) Lin Bloom McDowell, thank you for helping me to say what I needed and wanted to say. Editors are the invisible heroes that make creating a book possible.

Contents

Introduction

Of all the riches available to us in life, self-discipline is surely one of, if not *the,* most valuable. All things worth achieving can be accomplished with the power of self-discipline. With it we are masters of the energy we expend in life. Without it we are victims of our own unfocused and constantly changing efforts, desires and directions.

Self-discipline, focus, patience, and self-awareness are interwoven threads in the fabric of both true inner peace and contentment in life. Together, living in the present moment and being process-oriented is the path that leads us to these all-important virtues. This magical path is there for everyone. It offers its untold riches to us all. "The Practicing Mind" is about remembering what you already know at some level and bringing that memory into the present, where it will serve to both place you onto the path and empower you to partake in the journey.

Thomas M. Sterner

Everything in life worth achieving requires practice. In fact, life itself is nothing more than one long practice session, an endless effort of refining our motions. When the proper mechanics of practicing are understood, the task of learning something new becomes a stress-free experience of joy and calmness, a process which settles all areas in your life and promotes proper perspective on all of life's difficulties.

The Learning Begins

When I was a child, I studied the guitar, though I was so young at the time (4 years old) that I don't remember much of it. However, looking back on the music I played, it would be fair to say that I had acquired a fair amount of skill. I quit after two years and did nothing much musically speaking for the next several years. At the age of nine, like so many kids growing up, I began studying the piano. Once again, that lasted briefly, this time only ten months, and the reason for this was that I really didn't enjoy practicing. If asked why, I probably would have said that it was boring and difficult, and I felt as if I wasn't getting any better. Though my perspective at the time may have been accurate, it stemmed from the fact that I wasn't very good at the process of practicing music, or practicing anything else for that matter. Unfortunately for me, I was far from sophisticated enough to realize that. However, because of my love for music, I eventually returned to the piano and did go on to learn to play.

During my late teens and early twenties, when I was still single, I pursued music very seriously and achieved a fair amount of success. I could compose and arrange in just about any style. I played as a professional on many occasions, from the nicest country clubs to the worst taprooms. I put together a rather expensive recording studio and got to know some of the better known songwriters and artists in the musical world of pop, jazz and country. By the time I hit my mid-twenties, by most people's standards I was a pretty good musician.

My musical development continued, and by the time I

had reached my middle thirties, I began to realize that something had really changed in me with regard to my feelings toward practicing. I not only loved to practice and learn anything, but I found the total immersion of myself into an activity to be an escape from the daily pressures of life. I even felt cheated if I were deprived of the opportunity to practice something, such as a particular aspect of my golf swing. Much more importantly, what I was beginning to understand was that all of life is practice in one form or another. Until then, like most people, I mistakenly only associated the word "practice" with art forms such as music, dance or painting. I did not see dealing with a cranky child, an over-burdened work schedule, or a tight monthly budget as actions that required applying the same principles as did learning music. As my comprehension of this relationship between life, mental discipline and practice grew, I began to apply all of my effort into defining the fundamentals of the *practicing mind*, and into observing when and how often I applied these fundamentals in daily living. I wanted to better understand the changes in my perspective, which had created such a turn-around in my attitudes toward the process of learning something new. Had I just grown up and matured, or was it something more defined, something more tangible running in the background? I knew I processed life differently, but what were the mechanics of the new system? That was what I needed to know.

I didn't realize at the time that it was my experience of learning music growing up that had formed the foundation which would help me understand both the mental and spiritual struggles in which I now found myself as I searched for answers. Those early experiences, of wanting to accomplish something and having to deal with a personality that was not particularly well-disciplined at the time, went a long way in helping me understand how we fail at endeavors that may be very important to us. My successes and failures in music provided me with a point of relativity to which I constantly compared my daily experiences. That is why you will see references to music throughout the book. It is not, however, necessary that you yourself have studied music to feel a kinship with me as I describe the certain aspects of music that taught me so much. Since the nature of the *practicing mind* exists in all activities of life, you will no doubt be able to relate my experiences with others that you have had in your own life.

As important as music was to my learning process, it was not to supply me with my first inclination toward a personal change in how I approached daily life. I first became aware of my shift in perspective toward practicing when, on my wife's advice, I took up golf in my early thirties. I think initially, the reason I didn't see my early days of musical study as being a backdrop for this change in awareness was because those experiences were so far removed from the present day. Indeed, by this time in my life, music was second nature to me and the practice regimen was so natural that I didn't have the perspective of a struggling student any more. Golf, on the other hand, was totally new to me. I knew almost nothing about it and I had no preconceived ideas of how it should be played.

In the beginning, my father-in-law would take me out to play on his course, and I would rent or borrow some old clubs. I quickly learned the frustrations of the game, but what made a big impression on me was that I didn't see anybody playing who was really any good. Most of the people I observed had been playing golf for as long as I had been playing piano, and yet in their own activity they hadn't gotten out of book one, so to speak. They played terribly and seemed clueless as to how to fix their problems in the game. Perhaps my biggest advantage was that, even though I was not uncoordinated, I had not excelled in any sports growing up. Therefore, I assumed I would need to find an instructor to guide my learning process lest I end up like so many other eternally frustrated people in the sport. Also, because I had grown up trying to learn how to play musical instruments (besides guitar and piano, I also spent time studying the flute and saxophone), I *expected* it would take time and applied effort to master the skills that would bring both consistency and joy to playing the game. It never occurred to me that this would be a quick or easy study. I was undaunted by, but yet aware of, the fact that despite my ability to play the piano well, I had fallen short of many of my musical goals. I comforted myself with my knowledge that I was an adult now, armed with an adult mentality and all that I had learned from those failures. I was sure this would see me through to achieving my goals in this newfound endeavor.

What I learned from golf was that all of my failures in music had stemmed from my lack of understanding the proper mechanics of practicing, of the process of picking a goal, whatever that may be, and applying a steady effort toward achieving it. Perhaps most importantly, I realized that I had learned how to accomplish just that without the frustration and anxiety usually associated with such an activity.

Golf provided me with my first opportunity to quantify these mechanics into something tangible to someone with my upbringing; before this point, I was like everyone who had come before me. I wanted the joy and benefits that are rewarded to the individual who perseveres at working towards a lofty personal goal. I wanted to experience the self-discovery that one attains from picking a goal and steadily working toward it, regardless of the pitfalls and frustration. This desire to learn is only the first step, though. Without an understanding of proper practice mechanics and without an awareness of our own internal workings, we are almost assured of using up the initial inspiration and motivation which propels us into any endeavor, leaving us feeling we cannot reach the goal that had seemed so worth striving for just a short time before.

Why bother with any of this? This is a question I asked myself. I mean really, what is the relevance of this to how we live our life day to day? How does it impact what we experience moment-by-moment, what we accomplish, who we are? The answer is that it is everything. It is the blank page on which we draw our life. It determines not only what we draw but also what we are *able* to draw. It shapes every aspect of who we are, what we become and how we see others. It is self-discipline and self-awareness. It gives us patience with ourselves, with others and with life itself. It is certainly one of the most powerful and meaningful gifts we can give ourselves, and yes, only **we** can give it to ourselves.

Our culture today is one built on multi-tasking. This is not just for increased productivity (which never seems to be enough), but it is for survival. We teach it to ourselves, and we teach it to our children. We are always doing and thinking of more than one thing at a time. Think about the simple act of driving a car. What is the first thing many of us do after we start the car? We turn on the radio. Now we are driving AND listening to the radio. If someone is with us we are carrying on a conversation on top of that. If we are alone we are talking on a cell phone. Our minds are juggling many activities and our energies are very dispersed. Even though this tires us so completely, it has become normal for us as our world continues to move faster and faster. We don't even question the levels of absurdity it reaches at times.

Years ago I took one of my daughters to a skating party sponsored by the 6th grade of her school. I told her I would sit inconspicuously in the concession area and read while she skated. Here is what I saw and heard as I observed the scene. There were six television monitors hanging from the ceiling down along the main side of the rink where the people put on their skates. Each TV had a different channel playing and each one's volume was competing with all of the other TV's. There was loud music playing throughout the rink. There was a video game area where about a half-dozen full-size arcade machines were blaring out their own sound effects. There was also a seven-foot TV screen on one end of the rink playing a music video that was different than the music coming through the house PA system. Finally, there were all these eleven-year-old kids skating around the rink, and none of them were talking to each other. How could they? It was exhausting just standing there and absorbing all this sensory input that the mind needed to process.

At times we must do several things at once, but the problem for us is that we are so used to always multi-tasking that, when we decide we want to reel in our minds and focus ourselves on just one activity, we can't. Our minds are so agitated, and that agitation has a tremendous amount of momentum. It doesn't want to stop moving. It tires us out and stresses us out. We find we can't sit still, and we can't *be* still. However, the *practicing mind* is quiet. It lives in the present and has laser, pinpoint focus and accuracy. It obeys our exact direction and all of our energy moves through it. Because of that, we are calm and completely free of anxiety. We are where we should be at that moment, doing what we should be doing and completely aware of what we are experiencing. There is no wasted motion, physically or mentally.

Going back to the car example, how many times have you driven somewhere and then noticed that you don't remember a portion of the ride? This is because instead of focusing on driving the car, your mind was overflowing with unrelated thoughts. So few people are really aware of their thoughts. Their minds run all over the place without their permission, and they go along for the ride unknowingly and without making a choice. Instead of observing their thoughts and using their thoughts to serve them, they are *in* their thoughts.

If it weren't so tragic, it would be amusing. We are so convinced that because our technology is evolving, we must be doing the same. We think that because we have cell phones with cameras in them, we must be more advanced than someone who lived 2500 years ago; but in fact, those people in the past were much more aware of their internal world than we are because they weren't distracted by technology. We have all this technology, which is supposed to make our lives easier, and yet it doesn't. They had none of the technology but had much simpler lives and perhaps a better understanding of how their minds worked.

The Learning Begins

We think that our struggles today are only known to us, but they are timeless, and those that lived long before us faced the same internal struggles that we do. There is a story many centuries old that describes this struggle. The story is about a chariot rider who steps onto a Roman-style chariot drawn by four horses. In this story, the horses represent the mind. The rider with an undisciplined mind steps onto the chariot but has no hold on the reins. The four horses run wild all day, exhausting themselves and the rider as they both bump along off the chosen path, constantly changing directions. They know not where they are at any given moment or where they are going. The rider holds onto the railings and is just as helpless as the horses as they watch the scenery go by. However, the disciplined rider who has the reins in hand is in control and directs the horses down the focused, chosen path, whatever that may be. The horses have no will. Their energy is directed by the refined commands of the disciplined rider. The ride is smooth and they reach the desired destination in the least amount of time, with the least amount of effort and fatigue. Which would you rather be?

If you are not in control of your thoughts then you are not in control of yourself. Without self-control, you have no *real* power, regardless of whatever else you accomplish. If you are not *aware* of the thoughts that you are thinking in each moment, then you are the rider with no reins, with no power over where you are going. You cannot control what you are not aware of. Awareness must come first.

The quest of this book is to examine how we get from here to there. How did we learn to be the chariot rider with no hold on the reins, and what types of cultural habits or teachings reinforce and perpetuate that way of thinking? What can we learn from how kids think? What can we teach them so they have less to unlearn than we do? How do we do all this without struggling so much to accomplish it? These are the questions I asked myself and the ones I will hopefully answer for you.

When I began this project, I envisioned this to be a book that would help eliminate the struggles of learning to play a musical instrument. However, the further into the writing process I got, the more I realized that I was writing about my outlook on processing life, not just on playing an instrument or learning a golf swing. I realized that I was using what I had learned in the very process of writing the book. I observed my perspective on how I maintained my steady writing effort day to day. I saw its presence in the effort of trying to understand exactly what it was that I had learned and how to put that into words. I saw how I was able to run a very successful business and to be there for my young daughters. One day I noticed that I was feeling frustrated and somewhat irritated while I was taking care of my daughters. I was having all these ideas for this book but they were going to have to wait to be written down because my children needed my attention. I noticed that I had become the chariot rider who did not have control of the reins. I was allowing my mind to go off the path and work on the book instead of staying on the path and enjoying the time with my kids. When I realized this, I pulled in the reins, and let the book go until my next scheduled writing session. The stress disappeared immediately and I saw the fun I was missing by not being in the present moment with my daughters.

At its inception, I would not have been able to write "this" version of "The Practicing Mind" even if someone had sat me down and said, "I will pay your bills and look after your family, you just write." It took the writing process and observing myself going through the day to learn that.

I now realize that my approach toward moving through life began to change in my early twenties. Maybe this sounds familiar to you. Up until then I had a long list of interests that I had pursued with a lot of enthusiasm, but for which I had lost steam and energy relatively quickly. My biggest asset was that I was aware of the fact that I seemed to follow a particular pattern with regard to any new endeavor. First I would pick the particular activity, say exercising. Then I would really get involved in it by joining a gym and buying the proper clothes, etc. Then I would start the activity with a commitment to be steadfast, and persevere with my effort. After a few sessions, my initial enthusiasm would start to taper off and I would have trouble maintaining my interest and discipline. From that point, it would become harder and harder to continue with the practice of keeping up the exercising routine, and I would begin to make excuses to myself for skipping a session with promises like, "I will make it up on the next session or add one in the morning before work during the week." This was all folly, though, because I wouldn't follow through with these commitments either, and I would become more and more comfortable with letting things slide until I had completely gotten away from my original goals. There was also this nagging sense that I had let myself down, plus a feeling of not really being in control of my destiny because I wasn't completing something that I had made a decision to do. Eventually, in this cycle I would get to the point where I had lost all interest in the particular endeavor, and I would begin the search for the next thing that was going to fill the void in me, starting the whole process over again. But I was aware of this tendency and I would quietly observe myself participating in this routine with one thing after another.

Three things were happening at this point in my life that would prove to be the beginning of a major shift in perspective and awareness for me. First, I had begun taking piano lessons again from a teacher who was not only one of the best players in the area, but was only several years older than myself. Taking lessons as an adult proved to have a whole new set of advantages and disadvantages over studying as a child. We will go into these in a future chapter. Second, while in college, I had begun independently studying Eastern philosophies. My study at this point was fairly broad, not focusing on any one philosophy in particular, and was more a part of a self- imposed "religions and philosophies of the world" course. This would spark a contemplative process in me that, over the next 20 years, would forever change my understanding of the relationship between the mechanics of, and the reasons for, practicing anything. If you have never considered it, think about how everything we learn and master in life, from walking and tying our shoes to saving money and raising a child, is accomplished through a form of practice, something we repeat over and over again. For the most part, we are not aware of the process as such, but that is how good practice manifests itself when done properly. It carries no stress-laden anticipation of "when is the goal going to be reached?" When we practice anything properly, the fact that we are engaging in a difficult learning process not only disappears, but more importantly it dissolves into a period of inner calming that gives us a rest from the tension and anxiety that our "get it done yesterday" world pushes on us every day of our lives. For this reason, it is important to recognize and be in control of the process and to learn to enjoy that part of life's activity.

The third major influence on my shift in perspective toward learning anything new came from my career decision. I had decided to become a concert piano technician and piano rebuilder. This is a very unique vocation, to put it mildly. It takes years to learn the skills necessary to be a high-level concert technician, and even longer to become proficient at the art of fine instrument restoration. My days consisted of anything from preparing a $90,000 concert grand piano for a major world symphony performance, to painstakingly restoring a vintage grand piano back to better-than-factory-new condition. During my years in business, I worked for and met many of the world's best conductors, concert pianists, big band leaders, and pop, jazz and country-western singers, and restored pianos dating back to the Civil War period.

A grand piano action (which is the entire keyboard mechanism) consists of between 8,000 to 10,000 parts. There are 88 notes with about 34 different adjustments per note. A piano has between 225 and 235 strings, each of which has a corresponding tuning pin that needs to be individually adjusted at least once during a single tuning. The point is obvious.

The Learning Begins

Working on a piano is repetitious, tedious and monotonous to say the least. Everything you do to the instrument you must do at least 88 times. This forces you to let go of anything but the most practical and efficient attitude toward the daily work that faces you in the shop and on the stage. If you do not possess at least a minimal level of discipline and patience, your anxiety and frustration will soar.

My purpose in detailing the repetitive nature and monotony of this work is to give you an appreciation of why, out of sheer survival, I began to develop an ability to get lost in the *process* of doing something. As difficult as the job was, its monotonous nature enabled me to spend my day alone with my thoughts. This afforded me the time to observe and evaluate what worked and what didn't in terms of coping with the nature of the trade.

Throughout this book I will relate what I consider the key events and areas of my life that taught me so much about myself, why I struggled at times, why I let myself down at times, and how I moved beyond that, simply by observing some of life's simple truths.

And so, on to the beginning of understanding our *practicing mind.*

A paradox of life: The problem with patience and discipline is that it requires both of them to develop each of them.

2

Process Not Product

During the time I was studying golf, I participated in a 6-week group golf class. Each week, five of us, all adults, would meet at the driving range for an hour of instruction followed by an hour of practice on our own. At the beginning of the third session, I was sitting on a bench waiting for the class in front of ours to finish. Next to me was one of my classmates who had also gotten there early. I had learned on the first day when we had introduced ourselves that she was heavily involved in the corporate routine and wanted to learn golf for both relaxation and as a means of furthering her career. She explained that many times in the course of her job, golf outings were offered as a way of meeting new business contacts and discussing company matters in a relaxed setting.

As we chatted about golf and our jobs, I asked her this question: "Well, did you practice what we learned last week?" "No." she replied. "I had so much to do all week. I just want to wake up one morning and be able to play well." I sensed frustration and mild depression in her voice. She seemed frustrated that golf was much harder than it looked and depressed about all the hard work that lay ahead of her if she had any hopes of reaching the level of ability that she felt would make the game more fun.

When our class began, the instructor asked that same question of all of us even though he would know the truth as soon as we started warming up and hitting balls. I think the purpose of his question was to make us admit out loud whether or not we had found the discipline necessary to practice and habitualize the techniques that had been taught to us the previous week. *That* would allow us to easily move on to the next step. What was revealed was that only two of us had practiced at all during the week between sessions. One classmate had been to the range several evenings to go over what he had been shown. The remaining three had not only failed to practice, but had left immediately after the instruction period the week before instead of remaining to practice on their own. My weekly practice included the following.

After class the previous Monday evening I had stayed and hit balls for an hour to begin learning what had been shown to us during the lesson. Before leaving the range, I sat in the car and spent a few minutes writing down notes in a small journal I kept. I made sure that I had a description of everything we had covered in class. This was nothing elaborate, just reminders of the key points the instructor had discussed. During the week that followed, I would go into my basement to practice after my children had gone to bed and my wife and I had caught up on each other's day. I made a list of everything I would cover in that particular practicing session and divided it up so that I would be working on only one aspect of the golf swing at a time. In the course of going over each item, I would make anywhere from one to two hundred swings in front of a mirror with a short club I had cut off so it wouldn't hit the ceiling. I followed this up during the week with three trips to the range to actually hit balls, but again, only working on one part of the swing at a time. When at the range, I put most of my energy into ignoring what the ball flight looked like. I was in the *process* of learning parts of the golf swing. I didn't expect to be hitting good shots. A beautiful golf shot is the result or *product* of all the parts being correct.

To my classmates, this type of a practice routine would seem to require positively way too much time and effort out of their already over-burdened day. However, the reality was that, just as in learning a musical instrument as a child, I rarely put in more than an hour of practice time a day. Just turning the TV off would give the average person much more time than that. More importantly, I not only looked forward to the practice sessions, I needed them. They provided me with a diversion.

Just as for everyone else, my life was stressful at times and I looked forward to being absorbed by something that *wasn't*. Besides the normal ups and downs of family life, I had career deadlines to meet: expensive piano restoration work that clients had saved years for and wanted finished on time, regardless of whether some supplier had sent me the wrong parts or I had lost time to emergency service work for a symphony. I also had to deal with nerve-racking concert situations while preparing a piano for some of the biggest names in the music world. If there was a problem, I was the "go to" man. I had to provide the solution "right now," no excuses. At more than one symphonic concert, I found myself frantically searching for some nuance of perceived imperfection while the artist looked over my shoulder and a thousand people were kept waiting in the lobby for us to finish and clear the stage. Stress was no stranger to my job experience.

Contrary to what the other classmates were experiencing, I found that, when given my *present moment* attention, the practice sessions were very calming, not bothersome. I didn't have to be anywhere but "here," and I didn't have to accomplish anything but exactly what I was doing "right now." I found that immersing myself in the process of practicing would shut off all the tensions of the day and all the thoughts of what had to get done "tomorrow." It would keep my mind in the present, out of the past or the future. I would let go of any expectations of how long it would take me to acquire a good golf swing because I was enjoying what I was doing "right now," *learning* a good golf swing.

Why was I finding this an invigorating yet calming experience while my classmates were finding the opposite? I believe this was because I was actually practicing and they were not. Compounding the problem was their anxiety, which was created by their awareness that by not practicing, they were not getting any closer to their intended goal.

I believe they would have found the time and discipline and even wanted to practice if two things had occurred. First, they would have had to understand the mechanics of good practice. In other words, what makes the learning process efficient and free of stress and impatience? Secondly, they would have had to experience a shift in their intended goal. What I mean by this is that we have a very unhealthy habit of making the *product* - our intended result - the goal, instead of the *process* of getting there. This is evident in so many activities in our everyday life. We become fixated on our intended goal and completely miss out on the joy present in the process of achieving it. We erroneously think that there is a magical point that we are going to get to and then we will be happy. We look at the *process* of getting there as almost a necessary nuisance we have to go through in order to get to our goal. Let's look at both of the points mentioned above. What will become apparent is that they are really inter-related and that one creates the other. Let's define what the word practice means in its simplest form. To begin, we will look at the difference between practicing something and just learning it.

To me, the word "practice" and "learning" are similar but not the same. The word "practice" implies the presence of awareness and will. The word learning does not. When we "practice" something we are involved in *the deliberate repetition of a process with the intention of reaching a specific goal.* The words *deliberate* and *intention* are key here because they define the difference between practicing something and just learning something. If you grow up in a household where there is constant bickering and inappropriate behavior, you can *learn* that behavior without your knowledge. If that happens, then in order for you to change that behavior within yourself, you will have to be *aware* of the personality tendencies you possess, and practice a different behavior repeatedly and deliberately with the *intention* of changing. Practice encompasses learning but not the other way around. Learning does not take "content" into consideration. Keeping that in mind, we can also say that good mechanics require deliberately and intentionally practicing *staying* in the process of doing something and being aware of whether or not we are actually accomplishing that. This also requires letting go of our attachment to the "product".

The title of this chapter is "Process not Product". This simple and yet powerful statement is something I am sure you have heard in one form or another at some time in your life. Sayings such as *"stay on purpose," "don't be too results-oriented," "there is no goal in life, life is the goal,"* are all reiterating the same truth. What these are all saying is "focus on the *process*, not the product that the process was meant to achieve." It's a paradox. When you focus on the process, the intended product takes care of itself with fluid ease. When you focus on the product of your effort, you immediately begin to fight yourself and experience boredom, restlessness, frustration and impatience. The reason for this is not hard to understand. When you focus your mind on the present moment, on the *process* of what you are doing right now, you are always where you want to be and where you should be. All of your energy goes into what you are doing. However, when you focus your mind on where you want to end up, you are never where you are and you exhaust your energy with unrelated thoughts instead of putting it into what you are doing

In order to focus on the present, we must temporarily, at least, give up our attachment to our desired goal. If we don't give up our attachment to the goal we cannot be in the present because we are thinking about something that hasn't occurred yet...the goal. This is the goal shift I spoke of earlier. If you shift your goal from the product you are trying to achieve to the process of achieving it, a wonderful phenomenon occurs. All the pressure drops away. This is because, if your goal is to pay attention to only what you are doing right now, then as long as you are doing just that, you are reaching your goal in each and every moment. In one respect, this is a very subtle shift, and in another way a tremendous leap in how you approach anything that requires your effort. When you truly shift into putting your attention on what you are doing "right now" and continue to be aware that you are doing so, you begin to feel so calm, refreshed and in control. Your mind slows down because you are only asking it to think of one thing at a time. The inner chatter drops away. For most of us this is very contrary to how we handle most of our activities during the day. Our minds are trying to manage a whole list of things that we need to get done (future) or forgot to do (past). We are everywhere but where we are, and we are usually doing too many things at once.

This awareness of being where you are and in the present gives you the constant positive reinforcement of reaching your goal over and over again. However, when your mind is only on the finished product, you not only feel frustrated in every second that you have not met that goal, but you experience anxiety in every "mistake" you make while practicing. You view each mistake as a barrier, something postponing you from realizing your goal and experiencing the joy that reaching that goal is going to give you.

When, instead, your "goal" is focusing on the process or staying in the present, then there are no mistakes and no judging. You are just learning and doing. You are executing the activity, observing the outcome and adjusting yourself and your practice energy to produce the desired result. There are no bad emotions because you are not judging anything.

Using music as an example, let's say you are trying to learn a particular piece of music. If your goal is playing the entire piece of music perfectly, with each note you play you will be making constant judgments about the music and yourself. "I played that part correctly but I can't seem to get this part right." "Here comes the part I always mess up." "It will never sound the way I want, this is hard work." All these judgments require your energy, and none of that energy is going into learning the music and getting to a point where it is effortless for you to play it. These thoughts are only keeping you from learning the piece of music. We waste so much of our energy by not being aware of how we are directing it.

This doesn't mean that you lose touch with what you are aiming for at all. You continue to use the final goal as a rudder to steer your practicing session, but not as an indicator of how you are doing. This problem is present in any activity you choose because the final goal is usually the reason you undertake the endeavor in the first place, and it is always out there as a point of relativity with which to compare your progress. You can really see this dilemma in sports such as skating, gymnastics, bowling and golf, which have "perfect" scores, but in more subtle ways it is also present in all areas of life where we aspire to accomplish something. If, while writing this, I start to feel that "I just want to get this chapter done so I can move on to the next," I am doing the same thing. If you are trying to improve how you deal with a difficult person you work with, and one day you slip a little in your effort and then judge yourself for that, you are doing the same thing, It's everywhere in everything we do. In the particular case just mentioned, you would just stay in the present, observe your actions, use how you want to deal with the situation as a rudder, and adjust yourself so that you are in the process of moving toward that goal.

You could think of it as throwing tennis balls into a trash can from ten feet away. If I gave you three tennis balls and told you to throw them one at a time into a trash can ten feet away, you should perform the task something like this. You would pick up a tennis ball, look at the trash can, and toss the first ball. If the ball hit the floor in front of the can, you would observe this and make the decision to adjust the arc of the ball and how hard you tossed the ball based on this observed information. You would continue this process with each toss, allowing the present moment feedback to help you refine the art of tossing a tennis ball into a trash can.

Where we fall down in this activity is when we drop out of this present-minded approach and become attached to the outcome of our attempts. Then we start the emotional judgment cycle of "How could I have missed the first one, I am not very good at this, now the best I can do is two out of three," and on and on. If we stay in the *process*, this does not occur. We look at the outcome of each attempt with emotional indifference. We accept it as it is with no judgment involved. Remember, judgment redirects our energy and wastes it. It could be said that we have to judge the outcome of each attempt to make a decision on how to proceed, but this is not true. Judgment brings a sense of right or wrong, good or bad with it. What we are doing here is objectively observing and analyzing the outcome of each attempt. This observation serves only to direct our next effort. It is amazing how everything changes when we use this way of thinking to approach any new activity. For one thing, we become patient with ourselves. We are not in a hurry to get to some predetermined point. Our goal is to stay in this process and to direct our energy into whatever activity we are choosing at the present. Every second that we achieve this, we have fulfilled our goal. This process brings us inner peace and a wonderful sense of mastery and self-confidence. We are mastering ourselves by staying in the process and mastering whatever activity we are working on. This is the essence of proper practice.

Why are we so poor at all of this? How did we learn to process life in such a contrary manner that screams that the product is the only concern? This mentality pushes us harder and harder with no end in sight. By not staying in the process, all day long our minds are running all over the place, the horses running free with no one at the reins. We think too many thoughts at once, most of them the same thoughts we had yesterday and the day before. We are impatient with life and anxious.

We must accept that, to a certain extent, it is human nature. If you read about any of the great world religions and philosophies, you will find that at their core is the subject of our lack of ability to stay in the present moment. They all speak at great length about how overcoming this is everything in realizing and experiencing true inner peace and attaining real self-empowerment, hence the several-thousand-year-old story of the chariot rider.

In the West, we can blame at least a certain amount of our product orientation on the way our culture operates. This weakness in human nature is repeatedly taught to us and incorporated into our personalities. This makes it even more difficult to become aware of, let alone overcome, this crippling perspective. The idea that the end product is all that really matters starts when we are very young. Even if we do not remember exactly what behaviors we observed to instill this idea into our personalities in early childhood, it is surely there for most of us by the time we get to school age. If any of us are lucky enough to have failed to acquire this perspective before that time, you can be sure our educational systems will continue to work on its growth.

School is the beginning of what I will refer to as hard, fast *markers* that define who we are. These markers are of course grades. Grades, when functioning properly, should inform the educational system as to how well the present method of teaching is working. However, whether they actually accomplish this would seem to be up for discussion. Grades in school have been around for a long time, and people still get everything from A's to F's on their report cards. Standardized Achievement Tests or SAT exams are another form of grading our performance in academic matters. They heavily influence which colleges we are eligible to get into and whether or not the particular school will even consider us at all as potential students. During our school years our grade accomplishments define very much who we are and what we are worth. They can greatly influence not only how far we will go in life but in what direction we will head. They speak much to us about our sense of self-worth. Someone who scores mostly "Cs" feels like they are "Average". An "F" student is a "Failure", and an "A" student is, of course, "Excellent". During these years we begin to develop that bottom-line intelligence that states "results are everything" regardless of how we achieve them. Why else would people cheat?

I am not here to promote a new-age scoring system that makes us all feel like we are "head of the class" material. Besides being beyond the context of this book, it is also beyond my ability to do so. What *is* within the context of this book is how the grading system impacts our attitudes toward making the *product* the priority and not the *process*.

All through my school years I found math to be a most difficult subject. Even at a very early age, certain aspects of math just didn't make sense to me. The teacher would go over something new on the board and I would listen intently and try to follow, but to no avail. I would start on the new assignment with a resolve to overcome my lack of understanding with hard work, but it never seemed to help. I was very much a creative-minded child and not an analytical one in the mathematical sense. My grades always reflected this. Reading through my report card always showed I was somewhat of a "B" student with an "A" sprinkled in here and there, except for math. In subjects that were more right-brained, such as creative writing, I was usually the first one done. In math I was working after the bell had rung and most of the other students had left. Some of this was probably due to poor instruction. I say this because there *were* one or two math teachers who presented the material to me in a way that was very clear, and I could at least manage a B-C grade in the class, but that was the exception to the rule.

How this relates to our topic here is illustrated by what I learned about myself through the experience of school and grades. Most of us heard phrases during our school years that were actually rooted in the correct mindset of "process not product." I am speaking of encouraging words such as "just try your hardest, that's what is important" and "do your best, that's all anyone can ask." These phrases were very good advice, but somehow most of us knew they were empty, bogus statements. In regards to math I can honestly say I did try my hardest, but that never consoled me when I got my report card. I would immediately skip through the "C's", "B's", and "A's" that were scattered through the columns and go right to the "Math Comprehension" where the "D" (most likely a gift for trying hard) was sitting as big as life. I was very fortunate to have parents who were unimpressed with academic achievements. They were always encouraging despite the low grades I received. Still, in those elementary school days and all the way through college, I carried an inner perception that those grades were who I was and to some extent what my self-worth was, at least as far as math went. I learned to dread math of any kind and I felt inadequate in my ability to overcome that feeling.

I was not alone in this perspective by any stretch of the imagination. Some people, perhaps those whose parents were very much into academic achievement, had an even stronger commitment to the power of the grade. An example of this was when I took a music theory course at the local college. I was twenty-five years old at the time and living on my own. I had my own business supporting me and the decision to take the course was strictly my own. Because I was self-employed, I had the luxury of not having to take a night class. I could get right into the day class with the fresh-out-of-high-school kids.

One of the assignments in this class was to work on a computer. The computer program would test you on all of the material that was covered in class. It would grade you on each area of the work and it would not allow you to advance to the next lesson until you had passed the one you were presently on. What made matters worse was the "Big Brother" nature of the whole system. The computer lab was a room full of computers, as you would expect, but they were all tied into a central location. The professor could log into your lesson anytime he wanted to and see exactly where you were in the curriculum. This was before the days of the Internet and household networking, so the concept seemed very futuristic and somewhat daunting. If all this was not enough, you had a time element to work with. You were only allowed so much time to give each answer. What was particularly bad about this was that our class was unknowingly a test group. We were being timed, but the sister class covering the same lesson plan was not. We however did not know that we were the only ones with a time constraint on our answers.

I won't go into how I uncovered this secret, but what I learned was that someone in the college wanted to see if the students would learn the same material faster if put under a time constraint. This was an interesting idea, except that, since we were the first attempt at this procedure, the faculty didn't really know what a reasonable amount of time would be to give a student to calculate the answers to the computer's questions. They grossly underestimated, and no one was able to answer the questions in the time allotted. A right answer that took too long to type in was considered wrong by the computer, and hence a failure. Our frustration was worsened by the fact that the computer lab work counted as 33% of your final grade in the class.

On the first day of class, you received a schedule sheet describing what your expected progress should be on the computer on any given day. Virtually no one could even come close to meeting this schedule, and the farther behind you got, the more stressful things got. One day the professor made the mistake of stating rather casually that people were not keeping up with their computer work and reminding them to not forget the impact of this on their grade. The unexpected reaction he received was frighteningly reminiscent of the old westerns when an angry mob was hunting for a good rope and a tree to go with it. At this point, the faculty did not realize that they had put students in a no-win situation. They assumed that the time allotment was sufficient and fair and that the reason for the students' difficulties was that they were not putting in enough time. Students, on the other hand, were putting in way too much time and were even neglecting other classes in an effort to get this work caught up. Some of them were visibly distraught.

I was immune to all of this because I was an adult

student. I paid for my class and I really didn't care about the grade I received. I was only interested in information that would be helpful in my musical composing efforts. I didn't have to mail a copy of my grade home to my parents because I was on my own. Because I was older than the rest of the students, I also had the perspective that this class wasn't going to make or break my life. I had failed tests before and I was still here. I felt almost like a wizened parent watching children react to something that, to them, was so important and yet at some point down the road would seem so insignificant.

The point of this story was in how the students resolved the problem. In short, they cheated. They very blatantly cheated. Anyone could go into the computer lab at any time. It was open twenty-four hours a day, seven days a week and the professor was never around. Once the students found out what the questions were going to be, they would write down all the answers on a memo pad and walk into the lab, setting the pad on their lap. Before the computer finished asking the question they were typing in the answer. They got all their work caught up, had perfect scores, and felt very justified in their actions. Unfortunately, they learned little to nothing about music theory. While I would be sitting at a computer working on my assignment and talking to them, I would hear the same thing over and over again: "This class and this computer are not going to ruin my 'grade'." The *grade* was everything, the knowledge was nothing. They finished the course with a piece of paper that had a letter "A" on it that meant nothing. They had learned almost nothing during the three months (the process), but they felt like they had won because of the grade they had received (the product). But what did they really have that was of any lasting value?

On the other hand, what choice did they have? Our culture is a bottom line, results-oriented society. Corporations will hire a 4.0 before a 2.0 every time because they feel the 4.0 has more to offer. To them the 4.0 is who you are and what your future potential is. With regards to this particular incident, if someone had instead said "forget the grade" and expended all their energy on just learning as much of the material as possible, they would have had no valid way of representing what they had accomplished. Our culture does not recognize the value in being process-oriented, even though we see so much evidence for it in the work produced by countries that do.

Back in the mid-seventies there was a real upheaval going on in the business world of manufacturing. Everyone wanted a Japanese automobile because they were noticeably higher in quality. American auto manufacturers were scrambling to understand why this was and how to fix it. But this wasn't a situation localized in the auto industry. Japanese pianos were becoming popular in this country. Some of them had names people had never heard of and couldn't even pronounce properly, but they could see the quality difference in them regardless.

The Japanese were very process-oriented in their life and work. We had trouble competing with them because we couldn't duplicate their work environment or their whole mindset which was so different than ours. A major piano retailer that I performed service for related a story to me that really illustrated the primary differences between the two cultures. He had gone to Japan and taken a tour of the plant which manufactured a piano he sold in his store. While walking down the assembly line, he observed a worker whose job was to prepare the piano plate (the big gold harp assembly that holds all the strings) after it had come out of the casting. These plates are made from cast iron, and when they come out of the mold they are pretty rough looking. The plate must undergo grinding and polishing before it can be painted. The finished Japanese plates are absolutely flawless and beautiful. As the worker prepared a plate, my retailer friend asked him how many plates he could get finished in a day. The Japanese worker looked at him confused and answered "As many as I can make perfect." The retailer asked "But don't you have a supervisor to report to?" "What is a supervisor?" asked the worker. "Someone to make sure you do your job correctly," answered the retailer. "Why would I need some one to make sure I do my job correctly?" answered the Japanese worker. "That's my job."

We can't begin to conceive of a mindset like this. If it took all day to make one perfect plate, he had done his job correctly and fulfilled the company's expectations of his position. The job required him to focus his mind in the present and keep it there. By practicing this right thinking, he would produce the best work and would also maintain a fresh, uncluttered mind. One perfect plate was more important than twenty acceptable ones. The reason for this stemmed from the Japanese' understanding of the whole (product as the rudder) and their knowing that this patient approach would yield a much stronger result in the long run, which it did. They completely upset the automotive and music industries, not to mention the electronics industry as well.

We, on the other hand, can't wait that long for anything. We want the product and we want it now. Skip the process altogether and get to the product. We have become obsessed with having everything now. Credit card debt soars and ruins many people in this country because it feeds on this mindset of "get it now and pay for it later." Credit cards work on the premise of product *before* process instead of process first. This mentality only leads to a general sense of nonfulfillment and emptiness. We have all experienced a situation where we wanted something very much but didn't have the money for it, so we charged it. The fulfillment from attaining the object is usually gone long before the first bill for payment arrives. We have sayings that describe our addiction to this mindset. "Instant gratification" is one of them. But this would be more accurately stated as "Instant gratification - short term satisfaction" because anything we acquire of this nature has no real lasting value to us. You can recall everything you have worked hard and patiently for in your life, but how many things that you have attained with little or no effort can you remember? When we focus our energy on the process of attaining something, whether it be an object or a skill, and through patience and discipline we achieve it, we experience a joy that is just not present when something comes too quickly or easily. In fact, when we reminisce about whatever it was we were trying to acquire, the process is what comes to mind, not the object itself. We remember the mastery of our undisciplined nature, the patience and perseverance that we developed, and the joy and satisfaction we experienced then. What we discover is timeless because we experience it all over again.

I have no attraction for the first car that I worked and saved for all summer 25 years ago, but I can remember every detail of the work I performed to earn the money. I worked three jobs simultaneously. When my friends were off to the beach or lounging around, I stuck with it, and by the end of the summer I was the only one driving my own car. Once, when I was getting a little impatient to buy a car before I really had enough money, my father said something very profound to me. He said, "You are going to find out that buying the car is much less satisfying than working for it." He was right, and I never forgot those words. After I bought the car, it was somewhat of a let-down compared with the anticipation of owning it that I experienced while I was working toward the purchase.

This perspective is not just an individual one. Our whole culture participates in it at many levels and in many ways. Corporations are more interested in short-term profits than the long-term health of the company and its employees. Strangely, if you ask most people, they will agree that this is so, but we seem to be on a runaway train in this direction. We need to change this, and it starts within ourselves. Once we experience the shift to a "present moment, process not product" - oriented perspective, we know that it is right. We calm down. Our priorities adjust themselves and we feel peaceful and fulfilled with what we have and where we are. That age-old saying that "there is no destination in life, life is the destination" has real meaning.

So let's go back to my golfing classmates. What could

have changed their experience and motivated them to participate more in their goal of improving their golf games? If they had made the shift into a "process not product" mode, their mechanics would have followed. They would have been staying in the present and working on their swing with deliberation and an awareness of their intention. All of this would have changed their feelings toward working at their golf swing, and the false sense of "until I get this good, I am not going to enjoy or feel like doing this" would not have been present. The shift to the "process not product" mindset would have discarded those feelings, and instead of procrastinating their practice sessions, they would have looked forward to them.

In summary, it comes down to a few simple rules. Keep yourself process-oriented. Stay in the present. Make the process the goal and use the overall goal as a rudder to steer your efforts. Be deliberate, have an intention about what you want to accomplish, and be aware of that intention. Doing these things will eliminate the judgments and emotions that come from a product-oriented or results-oriented mind.

When you remain aware of your intention to stay focused on the present, it's easy to see when you have fallen out of this perspective. You immediately begin to judge what and how well you are doing and you experience impatience and boredom. When you catch yourself in that moment, just gently remind yourself that you have fallen out of the present, and feel good about the fact that you are now aware enough to recognize this. You have begun to develop the Observer within you that is so important with regard to the area of personal guidance. Understand that, while this will not be the easiest exercise you have ever undertaken, it is probably the most important. As I said earlier, all the major philosophies and religions have spoken at great lengths to the value of accomplishing this with regard to personal empowerment and inner happiness. Also remember the opening phrase if you do begin to succumb to discouragement. The paradox of patience and discipline is that it requires both of them to develop each of them.

As we attempt to understand ourselves and our struggles with life's endeavors, we may find peace in the observation of a flower. Ask yourself: at what point in a flower's life, from seed to full bloom, has it reached perfection?

3

It's How You Look At It

Most of the anxiety we experience in life comes from the feeling that there is a point of perfection in everything that we involve ourselves with. Whatever or wherever that perfection is, we are not. We continually examine everything in our lives, consciously or unconsciously, compare it to what we feel is the ideal, and then begin to judge where we are in relation to that ideal. Having a bigger home, more income, a certain kind of car, are all a normal part of this routine. The problem with these ideal images is that they may not be realistic or even attainable, and in general have nothing to do with real happiness. Our concepts of these images are handed to us by the marketing media. We watch all these perfect-looking people on TV and in the movies living their perfect lives. In television advertisements, this illusion is presented even more strongly: "Buy this and your life will be great," or worse yet, "Without this, your life is incomplete." Automobile commercials are particularly amusing with the strength of this message. They present ownership of their particular car as some sort of euphoric experience. In reality, we all know that cars are terrible investments that depreciate faster than anything else, and when we purchase a new one, we spend most of our mental energy worrying that it will be stolen or damaged in the local mall parking lot. Plus, while in the commercial they drove the automobile on some deserted back road full of farms, switchbacks and autumn scenery, we sit in a traffic jam on the expressway. Still, they continue to show us all the products we need to buy to complete our lives' yearnings, from cars to clothes to beverages.

You can learn a lot about yourself by watching the type of commercials that come on during your favorite programming. You can be sure the advertiser has spent a lot of money finding out what personality profile watches a particular type of programming before deciding what shows to sponsor. They also take it one step farther by stipulating what types of programming would attract an audience that will be receptive to their ad.

How we arrive at these ideal images of perfection, though, is not as important as becoming aware of how they distort our perspective of where we are on the road to happiness. If they are used for inspiration, they can be very beneficial; but if they are used as a measuring device, they become our downfall. For example, you could go out to a concert one evening and hear the performance of a world class piano soloist. The next day, so moved by the performance the night before, you could decide to take up the piano as an instrument. If you buy a CD of the soloist playing the performance you heard the night before and use it to give you motivation toward practicing, it could be a very good thing. If, however, you begin to analyze your progress based on where you are in relation to the soloist's performance (something that is usually done unconsciously), you are headed for discontentment and may even become so frustrated that you give up on your efforts.

If you don't believe that you do this, look more closely at yourself. We all do. That is why advertising works so well. It uses this nature in us that feels like "all is not right until I get to such and such a point." Whether that point is owning a particular item or reaching a particular status is not important. What is necessary in overcoming this nature is to become aware that we have the potential to perceive life in this manner and to know that our culture reinforces our tendencies toward it. We look in the mirror and judge our looks based on the present fashion trends and where we fit into them. Go out on a golf course and you will see somebody slamming a club into the ground because they missed a particular shot that may have been way beyond their ability. Their ideal and point of relativity, however, is the pro they watched on TV who hits 500 balls a day with a swing coach observing, and then plays five days a week. This is what I mean by unrealistic and perhaps unattainable ideal images. The amateur in question probably plays once a week, has had a few lessons, and maybe hits 100 balls a week. Yet his or her standard is the epitome of the sport.

We make a major mistake on the road to happiness when we adopt an image of perfection in anything. This is because an image or ideal is frozen and stagnant and limited by nature. It states that this is as good as this particular circumstance or thing gets. True perfection is limitless, unbounded and always in a motion of expansion. We learn a much more productive and satisfying perspective from studying the life of a flower.

The opening phrase for this chapter is the following: As we attempt to understand ourselves and our struggles with life's endeavors, we may find peace in the observation of a flower. Ask yourself: at what point in a flower's life, from seed to full bloom, has it reached perfection?

Let's look at this right now and see what nature is teaching us every day as we walk past the flowers in our garden. At what point *is* a flower perfect? Is it when it is nothing more than a seed in your hand waiting to be planted? All that it will ever be is there in that moment. Is it when it first starts to germinate unseen under several inches of the soil? This is when it displays the first visible signs of the miracle we call creation. How about when it first pokes its head through the surface and sees the face of the sun for the first time? All of its energies have gone into reaching for this source of life; until this point, it has had nothing more than an inner voice telling it which way to grow to find it. What about when it begins to flower? This is when its own individual properties start to be seen. The shape of the leaves, the number of blooms are all unique to just this one flower, even among the other flowers of the same species. Or is it the stage of full bloom, the crescendo of all of the energy and effort it took to reach this point in its life? Let's not forget that humble and quiet ending when it returns to the soil from where it came. At what point is the flower perfect?

I hope you already know that the answer is that it is *always* perfect. It is perfect at being wherever it is and at whatever stage of growth it is in at that moment. It is perfect at being a seed when it is placed into the ground. At that moment in time, it is exactly what it is supposed to be....a seed. Just because it does not have brightly colored blooms doesn't mean it is not a good flower seed. When it first sprouts through the ground it is not imperfect because it only displays the color green. At each stage of growth from seed to full bloom and beyond it is perfect at being a flower at that particular stage of a flower's life. A flower must start as a seed, and even though a seed holds within itself all that the flower will ever be, it will not budge one millimeter farther toward its potential grandeur of full bloom without the nourishment of water, soil and sun, but also *time*. It takes time for all of these things to work together to produce the "Flower."

Do you think that a flower seed sits in the ground and says, "This is going to take forever. I have to push all this dirt out of my way just to get to the surface and see the sun. Every time it rains or somebody waters me I'm soaking wet and surrounded by mud. When do I get to bloom? That's when I'll be happy, that's when everybody will be impressed with me. I hope I'm an orchid and not some wild flower nobody notices. Orchids have it all...no wait; I want to be an oak tree. They are bigger than anybody else in the forest and live longer too"?

As silly as this may sound, this is exactly what we do, and we do it, as they say, every day and in every way. We consciously or unconsciously pick a point of reference with regard to whatever it is we are doing and decide that nothing is right until we get to that point. If you step back and observe your internal dialogue from time to time during the day, you will be amazed at how hard you work against yourself with this type of thinking. When we are driving somewhere we can't wait to get *there*. Wherever *there* is, I doubt very much it matters whether we arrive fifteen minutes later 95% of the time.

When I am driving on the highway, all around me people are pushing the speed limit to the maximum and probably never notice most of what they drive past. When I look in my rear view mirror I see someone who is irritated with the world for getting in their way and exhausted by the stress and strain that impatience brings to the body and mind when we live in this state. If you step back routinely during your day and observe where your attention is, you will be amazed at how few times it is where you are and on what you are doing.

When you develop a *present-minded* approach to every activity you are involved in, and like the flower realize that at whatever level you are performing, you are perfect at that point in time, you will experience a tremendous relief from the fictitious, self-imposed pressures and expectations that only slow your progress. At any point in the day when you are involved in an activity and you notice you are feeling bored, impatient, rushed, or disappointed with your performance level, realize that you have left the present moment in your activity. Look at where your mind and energy are focused. You will find that you have strayed either into the future or the past. You may be subconsciously focused on the result or product you are trying to accomplish. This is usually found in activities that produce a tangible product, and could be anything from painting the house to losing weight. I would class this as a distraction into the future because what is pulling you out of the present and into the future is the product or result that you are trying to accomplish. You want to get to "full bloom" and skip the rest of it.

Sometimes, though, it is not a tangible thing that pulls us away from the present, but a circumstance. Imagine this. You are standing in your kitchen preparing dinner and your child or spouse is telling you about their day. Are you looking into their eyes when they are talking to you? Are you fully listening to what they are sharing with you in this present moment, or are you half listening while you anticipate going some place after dinner or thinking of something you said to someone at work that day that you regret?

Stop yourself during the day as much as you can and ask yourself "Am I practicing flower-like qualities and staying in the present with my thoughts and energies?" Nature knows what works because it does not have an ego to deal with. It is our ego that makes us create false ideas of what perfect is and whether we have reached it. As I said earlier, true perfection is not a finite thing. It is not a specific number, as in how much you weigh or how much you make. It is not a specific skill level that can be reached in an activity regardless of how long and how hard you pursue it. Ask any high-level performer in any sport or art form and they will tell you this. Their idea of perfection is always moving away from them, always based on what their present experience and perspective is. When we learn this truth we really get on the path to true authentic happiness. We realize that, like the flower, we are just fine, or rather we are perfect when we are where we are and absorbed in what we are doing right at that moment. With this perspective, we cease to be impatient to get to some false goal that will not make us any happier than we are right now.

We can learn so much from Nature by simply observing how it works through a flower. The flower knows it is part of nature; we have forgotten that. Remember, the reason we bother ourselves with such a life-long effort is not to be able to say "I have mastered the technique of present moment awareness." This is an ego-based statement. We work at this for one reason: it brings us the inner peace and happiness that we cannot attain through the acquisition of any material object or cultural status. What we achieve is timeless, always with us, and perhaps the only thing that we can really call our own. The stamina to pursue this attitude daily comes naturally when we realize that our present attitude has left us with a longing for something we can't seem to put our finger on. Despite all of our achievements and acquisitions in life, we still feel a longing for something to fill the emptiness inside. We may not have even consciously admitted this to ourselves, but the need for answers is still there. If it were not, we wouldn't be interested in reading material of this nature.

Present-minded awareness can be and is a natural process when the circumstances are right. We have all experienced this state of mind many times in our lives. The problem in identifying at what times we are functioning in this state is a paradox. When we are totally focused in the present moment and in the process of what we are doing, we are completely absorbed with the activity. As soon as we become aware of how well we are concentrating on something, we are no longer concentrating on it. We are now concentrating on the fact that we *were* concentrating on the activity. When we are practicing correctly, we are not aware we are practicing correctly. We are only aware and absorbed in the process of what we are doing in that moment.

In Zen this is referred to as "beginner's mind." Part of this is because, when you are a beginner at whatever activity you are attempting to learn, it takes all of your concentration to accomplish the activity and your mind is empty of chatter. As you become more adept at the activity, it actually becomes harder to concentrate solely on performing it. Remember when you first started learning to drive a car. You were totally absorbed in the process of learning to drive the car. You had a "beginner's mind." Now when you drive, you have lost that beginner's mind. You are listening to the radio, which you would have considered a distraction in the beginning. You are having a conversation with someone in the car or thinking of something you have to do later that day. Your mind is some place other than where you are, and on something other than what you are doing. The next time you get into the car, try to think of nothing other than driving the car. Try to keep your awareness on where other drivers are and what they are doing, what the scenery is, how your hands are placed on the wheel. If you are alone, try to stop any internal dialogue from going on and turn off the radio. It will seem maddening. You will find it impossible to give up your awareness that you are trying to *not* think of anything but driving the car. What was so simple and natural when you had no driving skills at all is seemingly impossible to repeat now that you are fully competent. The point of this is not to make us feel that we can't accomplish the desired mindset through effort, but to help us understand how we behave and feel when we are *in* it.

This is the true purpose of the martial arts. Hollywood has made the martial arts into a form of superhuman acrobatics whose goal is to take on any number of opponents and easily defeat them, but this is far removed from the original nature of the martial arts. The different forms of martial arts serve to teach the participant how to function in the present moment and to force them into this state of mind out of a desire for self-preservation. The student diligently works at all the different moves of the particular form he or she is studying. These moves are *deliberately* performed over and over again to a point of repletion with *intention* and *awareness*. They become totally reflexive and intuitive. When two students spar in a ring, the participants become completely focused on the present moment. They are aware of where they are in relationship to their opponent and what their opponent is doing. They observe each second as it comes at them and react instinctively to the motion of the opponent.

You can see how quickly you are made aware that your mind is wandering in a situation like this (you get hurt). There is no time to think of anything but the process of both offense and defense. In each second, you must be ready to both defend yourself or get out of the way of your opponent's advance and make your own strike if the opportunity presents itself. These sparring matches give the participants the opportunity to experience the instinctive total, present moment awareness that occurs during a life-threatening circumstance without actually being in any lethal danger. If you imagine yourself in a situation such as this, you will see how, during a present moment experience, you cannot be aware of anything other than the experience itself. This is why we cannot observe ourselves when we are practicing a process-oriented mentality. What we can do is use the moments of questioning whether we are focusing on the process to remind us that we are not.

Even though we cannot directly observe ourselves when we are functioning in a process-oriented, present-minded state, we can observe this state quite easily in others. One of the best examples of this is to watch someone play a computer video game. You will see perfect practice in action. Video games offer a natural environment for pulling us into a state of focused present moment awareness. In a video game, the score is essentially the end result or product that the player is working for, but the game itself is where the fun is. The process of playing the game takes all of your attention. If you take more than a second to glance at the score, it can make or break your attempt to beat the computer at the game. If you watch someone playing a computer game, you will observe how totally focused they are on what they are doing right in that moment. Even though the best score possible is the ultimate goal, the participant is only superficially aware of it. The process of playing the game requires all of their attention. If you talk to someone playing a computer game, they may not even answer you because they are so absorbed in the process of the game. Watching a movie can have the same effect on us if we find it particularly interesting. We say it captivates us because it captures our attention.

What is interesting about this is that most of us will find that, during recreational activities, we are very good at practicing properly. We perform the activity with all of our attention in the present and on what we are doing. What is the difference then between work activities and recreational activities? Why do we find it so much easier to focus on something we consider play than on something we consider work? If we could find the answers to these questions, it could be very helpful in advancing our efforts toward operating in that state all the time.

What I have found is that the only difference between the two activities is that we have pre-judged them. We have made a conscious decision that if we enjoy an activity it is not work. We must temporarily suspend our definition of work as referring to our daily vocation. "Work" in this discussion refers to any activity we don't feel like doing, and though it could certainly include our job duties or at least part of them, it could also refer to any activity that falls into the category of "undesirable." We know that this pre-judgment of whether an activity is work or play is not universal because one person's hobby is another person's drudgery. Some people love to garden, others don't even want to cut the grass. I watched a program one evening called "The Joy of Snakes." To me, that's a contradictory statement, but to the show's host it was absolutely true.

The knowledge that we pre-judge our activities and then place them into one of the two categories is very powerful. It demonstrates to us that nothing is really work or play. We make it into work or play by our judgments. The next time you find yourself doing something that you really don't feel like doing, stop for a moment and ask yourself why. What is it about the activity that is making you feel that way? You will find that many times you really can't put your finger on what it is that makes you feel that way. You will end up saying "I just don't feel like doing this right now." This implies that what you feel like doing is something else that you have defined as "not work." You are not in the present but instead are in the future anticipating another activity. But why, during a subconscious judgment process, do we define one activity as work and another as "not work"?

I feel that a large part of what makes us define

something as work is that the activity requires a lot of decision-making, and that can be very stressful and fatiguing. This is especially true when the decisions that you are making are very subtle and you are not even aware that you are making them. One time when I was performing a concert piano preparation for an orchestra and the soloist, I found myself going through the experience of "I just don't feel like doing this." As I tried to put my finger on exactly what it was that was making me feel this way, I realized it was the hundreds of decisions I was having to make during the tuning process and the responsibility that went along with them. When the soloist came out to perform that evening, all of his years of practicing and preparation were going to go out the window if I didn't set this instrument up correctly. The stress that was being created was from my concern about making the wrong decision, for which I would be held accountable. When I started to examine why I was lacking in confidence about something in which I had proven my expertise over and over again, I realized it was because I wasn't working in the present moment. I knew that I wasn't really giving my full attention to what I was doing. I was thinking about something I was going to do later in the day that I had defined as "not work." I subconsciously knew that I wasn't putting all of my energy into the process of what I was doing because, being so adept at it, I had lost that "beginner's mind" I mentioned earlier. I had tuned a whole section of the instrument and I couldn't remember doing it because I was in the future day-dreaming.

One evening I happened upon an interview with a well-known actor on television. I watch very little TV because I feel that most of it offers no return for the time you invest in it. But this particular interview caught my ear because I heard the actor talking about how he had gotten into meditating later in his life. The point of his interview in the context of this book is that he said he had become very present moment oriented. He found it increasingly difficult to plan future events because he was so wrapped up in what he was doing *right now* in *this* moment.

The main point he made in regard to what we are talking about here is that he had learned he could completely enjoy anything he was doing, provided he stayed in the present with his mind and just focused on the process of what he was doing right then. The difference this made in his life and how he felt was very profound to him.

Try this the next time you are faced with doing something you define as not enjoyable or as work. It doesn't matter if it is mowing the lawn or cleaning up the dinner dishes. If the activity takes a long time, tell yourself you are going to just work on staying present moment and process-oriented for the first half hour. After that you can hate it as much as usual, but in that first half hour you are absolutely not going to think of anything but what your are doing. You are not going to go into the past and think of all the judgments you have made that define this activity as work. You are not going to go into the future anticipating when it will be completed, allowing you to go participate in an activity that you have defined as "not work." You are just going to do whatever it is you are doing right *now* for half an hour. Don't *try* to enjoy it, either, because in that effort you are bringing emotions and struggle into your effort. If you are going to mow the lawn, then accept that all you need to do is cut the grass. You are going to notice the feel of the mower as you push it, how it changes resistance with the undulations of your front yard. You will pay attention to cut as wide a path as possible, not sloppily overlap the last pass you made as you gawk at the neighbor across the street washing their car. You will smell the cut grass and notice how the grass glows with green in the sunlight. Just do this for one-half hour of the activity. You will be amazed. Once you experience how the activity as mundane as mowing the grass is transformed, you will have the motivation to press on, because the potential effect this could have on your life and how you perceive it will become apparent to you.

I am not going to suggest to you that thinking this way is the easiest thing you will ever do, although as we discussed earlier, many times you do it naturally and without effort when you are learning something for the first time. At those times, though, you are not willfully doing it, and there is a difference. Whatever activity you choose to apply this technique to, it is best to begin with something you have no real emotions toward. If you suspect that you owe $5000.00 in taxes, choosing taxes as you first activity is probably not a good idea. The emotional content makes it that much harder. However, as you become better at it, you will realize that the whole value of this skill is in approaching these emotionally-laced activities and negating their negative power over you. The *practicing mind* puts you in control of even the most difficult situations and allows you to work with less effort and negative emotion in any activity. This means inner peace, and more accomplished with less effort.

In the next chapter we will begin discussing techniques for making this effort as easy as possible.

Habits are learned. Choose them wisely.

4

Creating the Habits We Desire

By now, you should realize, or shall we say be *aware* of, several themes running throughout this book. One of these themes is awareness itself. You cannot change what you are not aware of, and that truth is no more important than in the world of self-improvement. We need to be more aware of what we are doing, what we are thinking, and what we are intending to accomplish in order to be more in control of what we are experiencing in life. But in fact, for most of us, this is a problem because we are so disconnected from our thoughts. We just *have* them. The horses are running and we don't have the reins. We need to be more of an observer of our thoughts and actions, like an instructor watching a student performing a task. The instructor is not judgmental or emotional. The instructor knows just what he or she wants the student to produce. The teacher observes the student's actions, and when the student does something which is moving in the wrong direction, the instructor gently brings it to the student's attention and pulls the student back on the proper path. A good instructor does not get emotional in response to the student moving off the path. That kind of negative emotion comes from expectations, and that is not the perspective we want to have if we are to be our own instructor. Expectations are tied to a result or product; once again, we are experiencing the feeling of "things should be *this* way right now, and until then I won't be happy." When you or someone else is experiencing these kinds of emotions, it is an indicator of falling out of the process, or falling out of the present moment.

Like throwing the tennis balls into the trash can, we should observe, process the information without emotion, and then move on. This is how we should deal with ourselves as we work at learning something new, or when changing something about ourselves that we don't like. This includes working on something more abstract, like becoming more *aware* or conscious of what we are thinking: becoming more of an observer of ourselves.

This disconnection from our thoughts and actions is a way of thinking that we have learned during our lives, and it takes away all of our real power. We must unlearn this approach to life. What we are really talking about here are habits. Everything we do is a habit in one form or another. How we think, how we talk, how we react to a criticism, what type of snack we instinctively reach for, are all habits. Even when faced with a circumstance for the first time, our response to it comes from habit. Whether we observe our thoughts, or whether they just happen in our minds, is just a habit we have learned. We may consider some habits good, others not so good, but what is important to realize is that all habits can be replaced at will if you understand how they are formed. Habits and practice are very interrelated because what we practice will become a habit. This is a very important point because it underscores the value of being in control of our practicing minds. Our minds are going to practice certain behaviors whether or not we are aware of it, and what we practice is going to become habit for sure. Knowing this can work in our favor. If we can understand how we form habits and become aware of what habits we are forming, we can begin to free ourselves by intentionally creating the habits we want and not the other way around. We can gain control of who we are and what we are becoming in life. But what are the mechanics that create a habit? Knowing this would be quite valuable. Fortunately for us, we don't have to figure this out because others have already done it for us.

The formation of habits has been studied extensively by behavioral scientists and sports psychologists alike.

Understanding how desirable habits are created and undesirable habits are replaced is invaluable, particularly in repetitive motion sports such as golf or diving. In fact, you often see golfers practicing certain parts of their swing over and over again, or a diver standing poolside going through the motions of a complex dive they are about to execute. They are practicing and habitualizing their particular moves. What does that mean? To me, when we say that something is a habit, it means that it is the natural way we do something. We do it intuitively, without having to think about it. The martial arts student practices the moves over and over again, habitualizing responses that become effortless, intuitive, and lightning fast. There is no intellectual process that has to occur in a time of crisis where the brain is saying, "My opponent is doing this, I must do that." The responses just happen because they are a natural part of the person's behavior. That is what we are after. We want something like being more aware of our thoughts to be just a natural behavior to us, not something that requires a lot of struggle. Getting to this point is not complicated, but it does take some effort. The effort is minimal when we understand the process. What is required is that you are aware of what you want to achieve, that you know the motions you must intentionally repeat to accomplish the goal, and that you execute your actions with no emotions or judgments; just stay on course. You should do this with the comfort of knowing that intentionally repeating something over a short course of time creates a new habit and can also replace an old one.

The people studying this process in sports have gotten very comprehensive results. One study I am aware of states that repeating a particular motion sixty times a day over twenty-one days will form a new habit that will become ingrained in your mind. The sixty repetitions do not have to be done all at once, but can be broken up into, say, six groups of ten or two groups of thirty during the day, In sports, this type of method would be used to change a certain aspect of a golf swing or to naturalize any aspect of a sports motion. I shoot target archery. The way in which you draw the bow to full tension, and when and how you breathe, are part of good form. Practicing these proper motions so many times a day over so many days creates a habit of motion that *feels* right and natural and is done without conscious thought. However, you can just as easily haphazardly draw the bow and huff and puff, and that will also become a learned habit. That is why you must be aware that you are forming a habit, know what you want to accomplish, and apply yourself with intentional effort. Replacing undesirable habits works the same way.

I am sure you have experienced trying to change something that you have done a certain way for a long time. Initially, the new way feels very strange and awkward because you are moving against the old habit. But in a short period of time, through deliberate repetition, the new way feels normal, and moving back to the old way can feel strange. Once I learned this, the knowledge took so much of the stress out of learning something new for me. It became much easier to stay in the process of doing something, because I wasn't experiencing all the anticipation that results from not having any idea of how long it would take to learn something new. I would just relax and repeat the exercise and stay in the process, knowing that the learning was occurring. Yes, I was applying an effort, but there was no sense of struggle. I used this extensively in things like honing my golf skills or learning a new passage of music, but also in more personality-related changes.

When I identified something in my behavior that I felt was holding me back or producing undesirable results, I would realize that I had already fulfilled the awareness part of the equation. I would then objectively decide where I wanted to end up and what motions were going to get me there. Next, I would work at that process without emotion, knowing that so many intentional repetitions over a short amount of time were going to create the behavior I was after. There was no need to fret over it. I would just stay with it and know that I was where I should be right "now" and becoming what I wanted to be, accomplishing what I needed to accomplish.

It works very well, and the more you experience it working, the more confidence you have in your ability to shape yourself and your life into whatever you want. Being aware that all of your motions are habit, be they physical or mental, and that you have the power to choose which habits you will create, is very liberating. You are in control. Remember also that if you start to experience an emotion such as frustration, you have fallen out of the process. You are back in the false sense of, "There is some place other than where I actually am now that I need to be. Only then will I be happy." This is totally untrue and counter-productive. To the contrary, you are exactly where you should be right now. You are a flower.

All the patience you will ever need is
already within you.

Perception Change Creates Patience!

My mother, who passed on from cancer a number of years ago, expressed to me an observation she had made about herself as she sorted out both her illness and her situation in her mind. It is worth passing on here. During the time she was dealing with her illness, she was reading through some books that served to both comfort her and to make her more aware of her spiritual nature. This daily routine gave her a soothing perspective during what was surely a difficult time. Though she tried to keep up with this routine, there were times, for whatever reason, when she would drift away from both the reading and thinking about what she had read. She told me one day that when she kept up with her effort, her whole thought process was elevated and more evolved. She felt different about herself and life, and she had more clarity and perspective about her situation. But she also noticed that when she drifted away from her reading and fell into an, "I don't have time or don't feel like it today" frame of mind, she would feel herself slip back into an attitude and perspective that she felt was not only unproductive, but unfortunately very prevalent in the world today. Speaking about what she was reading, she said, "You need to keep reviewing these ideas so that you can hang on to the clarity and perspective. Otherwise, life steals it away."

I took something from that when I was writing this book. There are not that many ideas in this book - just a few, and they have always been there for us to discover. But they slip away from us in our daily lives so easily. They need to be reviewed over and over again from different angles so that they become a natural part of us. We are practicing learning them right now.

Sometimes when I read a book, I can't read it straight through because of my schedule. Instead, I may read two chapters today and another one three days from now. I have noticed that when this happens, I often can't remember points that were made earlier in the book which, when I read them, I felt were very valuable. I wanted this to be a book that you could pick up at any time and open to any page, start reading, and remember those few ideas without much effort and without the need to flip back through pages to find them. I wanted you to realize that we keep coming back to the same few solutions to all the problems we feel we have, and begin to realize that life isn't as complicated as we had thought. Changing our experience of life is well within our grasp, but we have to review a few ideas again and again so that everyday life doesn't steal them away before they become a natural part of who we are and how we operate. That is why I reiterate those ideas throughout the book. I also wanted to bring out the interrelationship of these few concepts and many of the virtues we all would like to possess. Patience is a good example.

Patience is probably at the top of everyone's list of most sought-after virtues. Patience is defined in the dictionary as "quiet perseverance." I would agree with that, but it also contains a quality of calmness that marks its outer appearance. Why is patience so hard for us to achieve in life? I am speaking of patience in general, whether we are dealing with a traffic jam, dealing with someone else who is having a bad day, or showing ourselves patience as we work at the ideas in this book.

It might be easier to come at this from an angle of impatience because we all are more familiar with the feeling of being impatient. We notice when we are impatient because we experience negative emotions. If you think about it, when you are being patient about something, life just seems fine. There is certainly no anxiety linked to being in a patient state. When you find yourself being impatient about something, what you are experiencing is completely different.

Experiencing impatience is one of the first symptoms of not being in the present moment, not doing what you are doing, and not staying process-oriented. I feel that staying in the present moment is one of the hardest lessons to learn. We are always dropping out of the "now" and letting our minds lead us around by the nose to who knows where. I have observed my mind many times through listening to my internal dialog. It goes from one totally unrelated discussion to another. It's thinking of a sharp-witted comeback I should have made yesterday when someone irritated me, reminding me to pay a bill, writing a musical piece, solving a problem, etc. All of this is going on while I am taking a shower in the morning. In that moment, my mind is everywhere but where I really am - in the shower. My mind is anticipating circumstances that haven't happened yet and trying to answer questions that haven't even been asked. We have a name for this: it's called worrying. If you force your mind to stay in the present moment and to stay in the process of what you are doing, I promise you, so many of your problems will melt away.

There is a saying that states that most of what we worry about never comes to pass. Thinking about a situation before you are in it only scatters your energy. "But," you say, "I have a difficult meeting with someone tomorrow and I want to have my thoughts together before I get into the situation." Fine, then take half an hour to sit down in a chair and do nothing else but go through the meeting in your mind and be there completely, doing only that. In the calmness of that detached moment, when you are not emotional, think of what you are going to say and anticipate the different combinations of responses the person can make. Decide on your responses and see how they feel to you. Will these responses have the desired affect? Now you are doing nothing else but what you are doing. You are in the present and in the process. You aren't scattering your energy by trying to act out all of this in your head while you are eating your lunch or driving to work. This constant inner dialog chattering away brings with it a sense of urgency and impatience because you want to deal with something that hasn't occurred yet. You want to get it done.

The first step toward patience is to become aware of when your internal dialog is running wild and dragging you with it. If you are not aware of this when it is happening, which is probably most of the time, you are not in control. Your imagination takes you from one circumstance to another, and your different emotions just fire off inside of you as you react to each problem it visits. To free yourself from this endless and exhausting cycle, you must step back and notice the real you, the Observer that just quietly watches all of this as it is happening. As you practice staying in the present, you will become more aware of the difference between the real you and the ego's internal dialog, without trying to do so. It happens automatically for you. Staying in the present and in the process is the first part of the equation that creates the patience that leads to a change in perspective.

The second part is understanding and accepting that there is no such thing as reaching a point of perfection in anything. True perfection is both always evolving and at the same time always present within you, just like the flower. What you *perceive* as perfect is always relative to where you are in any area of your life. Consider a sailor trying to reach the horizon. It is unreachable. If the sailor sees the horizon as the point he must reach to achieve happiness, he is destined to experience eternal frustration. He works all day at running the boat, navigating, and trimming the sails, and yet by nightfall he is no closer to the horizon than he was at dawn's first light. The only reference he has to forward motion is the wake left behind by the boat. Unseen to him are the vast distances he is really traveling just by keeping the wind in the sails and applying the moment-by-moment effort of running the ship.

Look at the things you feel you need to create the perfect life, and carry them through in your mind. Perhaps it is more money. That's the biggest falsehood ever perpetrated by humans. When does anyone ever have enough money? The wealthiest people in the world only want more and worry about losing what they have. There is absolutely no peace in this way of thinking. The feeling of "I'll be happy when" will never bring you anything but discontentment.

There is an endless nature to life. There is always more to be experienced. Deep down we know this and are glad for it. The problem is that everyday life steals this from us. It pulls us away from this perspective with a constant bombardment of advertisements all promising to fulfill us, but none of it ever works: "Get this, do that and life will be perfect." We need to let go of this futile idea that happiness is out there somewhere, and embrace the infinite growth available to us as a treasure, not something that we are impatient to overcome.

People involved in the arts understand this endless nature through direct experience. It is part of all the arts. That is why I believe that a personal pursuit in some form of art is so important to a person's sense of well-being. It teaches you this true nature of life right up front if you pay attention. When I was in my late teens, there were two incidents that created so much more patience within me as a result of a change in my perception.

The first happened shortly after I had started studying jazz improvisation with perhaps the best jazz pianist in the area. His name was Don. After one of my lessons, Don started playing around on the piano as I was packing up my music. I had never met anyone who played the piano as well as he did. He had earned his ability with years of a solid practice ethic, working at the piano sometimes seven and eight hours a day. While he was playing, Don told me that he felt that if he didn't start working harder he was never going to get really good on the piano. I was shocked by his casual remark. I commented to him that if I could play the piano as well as he could, I would be content to sit all day long and do nothing but listen to myself play. He looked at me and smiled. "You know, Tom," he said, "that is exactly what I said to my teacher years ago when I first heard him play." Don had studied with a world-renowned classical and jazz pianist. I had heard recordings of his teacher, who was extremely accomplished. Still, it occurred to me that if someone could reach Don's level of playing ability and still feel unfulfilled, I was going to have to re-think both my motivations for studying the instrument and my feeling the need to reach some level of "perfection" in order to become fulfilled.

The second event grew out of the first and began when I was nineteen years old. I had been studying with Don for just over a year. I was trying to play a certain passage in a piece of music and wasn't having much luck at it. I was frustrated and feeling a bit sorry for myself for not measuring up to my own standards. I wasn't progressing fast enough in my mind. I made the decision that I would write down all that I needed to accomplish musically to meet my own criteria of good musicianship. The list included items such as being able to play fluently in certain difficult keys, playing in front of large audiences, etc.

Several years later I was working in a small practice room at college late one night and I was having another difficult practice session. I remember thinking to myself that I was never going to get any better no matter how hard I tried. Depressed, I decided to quit for the evening. As I started packing up my music, a crumpled-up slip of paper fell out of one of my music books. It was the five-year music plan I had made when I was nineteen years old. I was twenty-two now and I had completely forgotten about it. I sat down and began reading the list to myself. What I read took me by surprise and made a lasting impression. I had accomplished everything on the list in less than three years, not five. In fact, I had done things musically that I couldn't even imagine doing when I was nineteen, and yet I didn't feel any different. I didn't feel any happier with my music or any better as a musician. My horizon was moving away from me. My concept of a good musician was coming from a different frame of reference. In that moment I had a realization which took several minutes to fully evolve. I became aware that there was no point of musical excellence out there that would free me from the feeling of "I need to get better." In that moment, I understood that there was no point I could reach where I would feel that I had finally done it, that I was as good as I needed to be, and that there was no need to improve because I had arrived at my goal. It was an epiphany. At first I felt a moment of overwhelming depression and fear, but it was immediately followed by joy and relief of the same magnitude. I knew that what I was experiencing was a realization that all true artists must go through. It was the only way to build the stamina necessary to continue in an infinite study.

There was a sense of freedom in knowing that I would never run out of room to grow. There was a peace in knowing the race was over. Where I was "right now" was just where I should be for the amount of effort I had expended. I saw the wake behind the boat for the first time and realized I was moving ahead, pretty quickly as a matter of fact. But the most important truth revealed to me in that moment was this: the real joy was in my ability to learn and experience that growth moment by moment. The process of discovering the ability to create music that had always been within me was the goal, and I achieved that goal in every second I was practicing. There were no mistakes being made, just a process of discovering what worked and what didn't. I was no longer struggling up a mountain toward some imaginary musical summit that was going to make my life complete. I realized the infinite nature of music and I was relieved instead of intimidated or frustrated.

That moment was the beginning of my shift in awareness of how I approached anything in life which required applied effort over long periods of time. That subtle shift in perception, and that is all it was, brought about unlimited patience with myself. I became patient with my progress. I not only stopped looking *at* my progress, I stopped looking *for* my progress all together. Progress is a natural result of staying focused on the process of doing anything. When you stay on purpose, focused in the present moment, the goal comes to you with frictionless ease. However, when you constantly focus on the goal you are aiming for, you push it away instead of pulling it toward you. In every moment of your struggle, by looking at the goal and constantly referencing your position to it, you are affirming to yourself that you haven't reached it. You only need to acknowledge the goal to yourself occasionally, using it as a rudder to keep you moving in the right direction.

It's like swimming across a lake toward a large tree on the other side. You should focus on just keeping your head down and pulling the water past you with each stroke. You fill your lungs with fresh air and then expel it in a relaxed fashion, glancing at the position of the tree on the distant shore every so often to keep your sense of direction. You do this with total detachment, or at least as much as you can muster. You say to yourself, "Oh, I need to steer a little to the left, that's better." If, however, you try to keep your head above the water the whole time, watching the tree and trying to see how much closer you are to it after each stroke and kick, you waste enormous amounts of energy. You become frustrated, exhausted and impatient. You become emotional and judgmental about your progress and you lose your stamina. All of this energy you are wasting could be going into reaching the far side of the lake, but instead you are dissipating it through incorrect effort, which produces negative emotions. You are fighting yourself and pushing against the task. It will take you longer to reach the tree on the far side of the lake if you reach it at all.

We have seriously missed the boat with this whole concept in our culture. We not only take the opposite path to an extreme, but we are so infatuated with reaching the goal of our efforts that we miss the point entirely. Here are just two examples that will further illustrate this.

In the early 1970's, you could go to any mall in the country that had a music store, and there would be someone demonstrating what I will call a self-playing organ. These instruments were designed for people who wanted to learn how to play the organ and wanted to play it "right now." They didn't want to spend "years of practice" to do it. The organ manufacturers saw this as an opportunity, and set about to exploit it by designing a keyboard that would tap into that personality.

In case you were never exposed to one of these cheesy keyboards, they worked like this. Usually, you pushed one key with the left hand and one with the right, and the organ played a full arrangement of the particular song you had selected. The organs came with all of the popular music of the day, and oldies too. That music showed you which note, and I do mean one note, to push with each hand to play your favorite song. In short, the keyboard knew how to create the accompaniment for the piece based on which keys you were pushing down. You played one note in the right hand, and it would create the chords needed to make the song sound like you had practiced long and hard. Since you only needed two fingers to play, you could have played entire arrangements with a pair of chopsticks. Did they sell? Certainly. People loved the idea of impressing their unknowing friends with how well they could suddenly play. The sales people who demonstrated them could also play for real, though that wasn't normally discussed, even as they added a few extra notes here and there. Even if the customer noticed that, they wanted to believe they could play instantly, so they ignored it. They would push one note here, another there and the organ would produce a performance equivalent to, say, an intermediate student. The whole time they would be exclaiming "I can really play." "No, you can't," I used to think to myself. "You aren't really playing. The organ is playing and it's having much more fun than you can ever imagine."

The point here is obvious, but many of us don't see it. Cheating discipline doesn't work. The people who bought these organs, hoping to experience playing, didn't understand that pushing buttons is not the same as playing, and no matter how many buttons they would push, they still wouldn't know what it felt like to play music. To sit and express a melody on any instrument as it comes from your heart is an experience you have to earn. The Universe is not about to give that away for anything but your personal effort. As you work at the process of learning music, you spend time alone with yourself and the energy of music or whatever art form you are working in. It's a very honorable relationship, really. You need music to express yourself and music needs you to be expressed. You give your time and energy to music and it returns the effort a thousand-fold. A lot of the joy in the experience of expressing yourself musically is your awareness of how much of your personal energy and stamina it took to reach whatever level of performance you are capable of.

I think it is fair to assume that we all know this universal law at some level of our being. Whether you are persevering at a diet, exercising regularly, running a marathon, or achieving any personal goal, if it comes with little or no effort, it means nothing. That is why these keyboards just fell away. In my business I would see these organs in people's living rooms gathering dust. Not once did I see them being played. That's because the experience of playing them was shallow and boring. What is sad about this to me is that the people who purchased the keyboards may actually have begun to feel that learning and playing a musical instrument wasn't as magical as they had once thought.

The second example is one we all know as credit cards. Credit cards, though convenient and certainly necessary at times in the modern world, are a form of instant gratification, but perhaps they should be called insignificant gratification. Credit cards allow you to jump to the end result without any effort. You can easily purchase anything you want without having to work or wait for the necessary financial energy that ownership of the object calls for. They even allow you the luxury of excusing yourself for not waiting as you promise yourself you will pay the bill off at the end of the month when the statement comes. Some people do this, of course, but most do not. That is why you see an ever-rising rate of people in trouble with the credit card debt they have created for themselves.

Like the self-playing keyboards, credit cards give you the feeling that you are cheating patience out of making you wait for something. "I want it now and I will have it." It is easy to hand over the plastic and it is much more convenient than carrying cash. You aren't even aware that if you don't pay it off inside the grace period, what you are purchasing is costing you perhaps 18% more than the price tag on it. People tell themselves they will pay it off, but most times they don't. Long before the bill arrives, the excitement of acquiring the object has worn off. Why? Because it came with no effort. We are back to that universal truth that just won't go away, so we may as well accept it and learn to use it to enhance our life instead of pushing against it.

The real thrill in acquiring anything, whether it is an object or a personal goal, is in anticipating the moment of receiving it. The real joy lies in creating and sustaining the stamina and patience needed to work for something over a period of time. Like swimming across the lake toward the large tree, we focus on each moment of our effort toward the object, only acknowledging the object to ourselves occasionally to maintain our energy and direction. When the time comes to actually acquire it, we have generated a tremendous amount of energy. We have earned the privilege to acquire the object, and that acquisition is the culmination of our entire process: the discipline, the work, the restraint and patience and finally the holding it in our hand. The reward of the whole is so much larger than just getting it with a phone call or plunking down a card that requires no effort.

So many people miss this point. They look at the process of working for something as an annoying effort they have to go through to get what they want. They make getting the "thing" the goal instead of "getting there" the goal. "Just getting the thing" produces a very small return investment of inner joy compared with the process of "getting there and achieving the goal." The key word here is "achieving." To me, *getting* the goal and *achieving* the goal are worlds apart. Most people spend their lives on an endless treadmill where they acquire or get one thing after another with no experience of lasting joy or personal growth.

To change your perspective, you must first realize this truth, and secondly, you must become aware of when you are involved in the process of working toward a particular goal. When you make a decision to acquire something which will require a long-term commitment, pick the goal and then be aware you are entering the "process" of achieving the goal. You cannot do this if you are constantly making the end result your point of focus. You have acknowledged the goal, now let go of it and put your energy into the process of achieving the goal.

When you let go of your attachment to the object you desire and make your desire *the experience of staying focused on working toward your goal*, you are fulfilling your desire in every minute and you are patient with the circumstance. There is no reason not to be. There is no effort or "trying to be patient" here. It is just a natural response to your perspective. This shift in perspective is very small and subtle on the one hand, but it has enormous freeing power. No task seems too large to undertake. Your confidence goes way up as does your patience with yourself. You are always achieving your goal and there are no mistakes or time limits to create stress.

To use music once again as an example, suppose you are trying to learn how to play a piece of music and you come from this new perspective. Your experience will be totally different than what we usually think of in terms of learning to play a musical instrument. In the old way, you are sure that you are not going to be happy or "successful" until you can play the piece of music flawlessly. Every wrong note you hit, every moment you spend struggling with the piece, is an affirmation that you have not reached your goal. If, however, your goal is *learning* to play the piece of music, then the feeling of struggle dissolves away. With each moment you spend putting effort into learning the piece, you are achieving your goal. An incorrect note is just part of learning how to play the correct note; it is not a judgment of your playing ability. In each moment you spend with the instrument, you are learning information and gaining energy that will work for you in other pieces of music. Your comprehension of music and the experience of learning it are expanding. All of this is happening with no sense of frustration or impatience. What more could you ask for from just a shift in perspective?

The final chapters in this book are techniques I have learned from all areas of life to help you make the shift in perspective that can be a challenge to our Western mind. These techniques are simple to understand, and I have tried to define most of them with one or two key words. I have found that by doing this, it is much easier to recall them during the day when you are involved in a situation that becomes frustrating. You will find that by reviewing them from time to time, the ideas will help you deal with the constant "product rather than process" orientation so prevalent in our culture. Let's get to them.

Simplicity in effort will conquer the most complex of tasks.

6

The Four "S" Words

The four "S" words are *Simplify, Small, Short, and Slow.* As you will see, these components are very interrelated and flow back and forth into one another. As you work on developing control of your practicing mind, it is important to work in a fashion that makes staying in the process as easy as possible. When you work at a specific project or activity, *simplify* it by breaking it down into sections. Don't set goals that are too far beyond your reach. Setting unrealistic goals creates frustration and invites failure. This can make you doubt your abilities. The success of attaining short-term goals will generate motivation that propels you along in the process, and you won't suffer the mental fatigue you experience when you bite off more than you can chew.

Be aware of what your overall goal is, and remember to use it as a rudder or distant beacon that keeps you on purpose. Break the overall goal down into *small* sections that can be achieved with a comfortable amount of concentration. You will find that focusing on small sections is so much easier and gives you repeatable success. These techniques apply to daily life in general, not just specific endeavors. They apply just as much to a fitness program as they do to cleaning the garage on Saturday afternoon, or developing a perspective change that affords you more patience.

If you look at the example of cleaning the garage, you see an activity that most would consider worthy of full-scale procrastination. But when it has to be done, step back and examine your feelings toward the job. You will find that your tendency is to see the necessary work-energy in its entirety. You see the whole task ahead of you and it looks huge. This viewpoint brings about a lot of judgments and negative emotions. You are full of anticipation as you find yourself saying things like, "There are so many things I have to move. Should I keep this or get rid of it? Will I ever need that thing over there again? The whole garage is a mess and that means lots of time, lots of energy and lots of decisions I don't feel like making after a week of work. I just want to relax." All of this internal dialogue has nothing to do with cleaning the garage and yet it is exhausting you.

You simplify the task so much when you break it down into small sections. "I am going to start in this corner over here and clean just to the window, that's all. I am not going to concern myself with the stuff over by the door or up in the rafters. Just this corner right now is all I am going to contend with." Now you're dealing with something that doesn't have the overwhelming qualities of the whole job.

Now you can also bring *short* into the equation. "I'm going to work at this project of cleaning the garage for forty-five minutes a day over the next few days until it is completed." You can survive just about anything for forty-five minutes. Now you only have to deal with this corner of the garage for forty-five minutes and you're done for the day. You look at your watch and walk away from the task at the end of the forty-five minutes, feeling in control and satisfied that your goal of a clean garage is flowing toward you. There is no frustration involved. You have simplified the task by breaking it down into small segments and only asking yourself to focus for a short period of time. You are practicing the art of perfect garage cleaning.

Incorporating *slowness* into your process is a paradox. What I mean by slow is that you work at a pace that allows you to pay attention to what you are doing. This pace will differ according to your personality and the task in which you are involved. If you are washing the car, you are moving the sponge in your hand at a slow enough pace that allows you to observe your actions in detail as you clean the side of your car. This will differ from, say, the slow pace at which you will learn a new computer program. If you are aware of what you are doing and you are paying attention to what you are doing, then you are probably working at the appropriate pace. The paradox of *slowness* is that you will find you accomplish the task more quickly with less effort because you are not wasting energy. Try it and you will see.

Another interesting aspect of deliberate slowness is the way it changes your perception of time passage. Because all of your energy is going into what you are doing, you lose your sense of time. In my business, sometimes the demand for my personal skills far exceeded the hours I could work in a day. I worked many seven-day weeks and sometimes fourteen to sixteen hours a day for long stretches of time. Once, when I had a particularly long day of service ahead of me, I decided I was going to put all of my effort into deliberately working slowly. It may sound like a contradiction to think this way, but I had been putting in way too many hours on the career end of the equation and my life was out of balance. I was tired and frustrated. If I couldn't get a day off, then at least the idea of going slowly for one day seemed rather appealing to me. I was to start with a concert preparation on a grand piano for a guest soloist of the local symphony. I was to prepare the soloist's piano in the morning along with a second piano that would be used in the orchestra. From there I had service work that covered two states, and then had to return to the concert hall that evening to speak with the soloist and check the two pianos once again. The workload was about two and one half times the amount that was considered a full day's schedule in the trade. I use the word "schedule" here because I was on a time schedule: Be "here" at 7:30 a.m. and "there" by no later than 10:00 a.m., etc.

When I started on the first piano, I put all of my effort into "being slow." I opened my tool box very slowly. Instead of grabbing a handful of tools and thinking I was saving time, I took each tool out one at a time. I placed each tool neatly in position. When I began setting up the piano, I performed each process individually, trying to deliberately work slowly.

It's a funny feeling when you try this. At first, your internal dialogue is howling at you to get going and pick up the pace. It is screaming at you, "We'll never get this done, you are wasting time." It is reminding you of the whole day's worth of work you have to get done to meet everybody's approval. You can feel the anxiety start to build and the emotions floating up to the surface. However, your ego quickly loses ground to the simplicity of doing one thing at a time and doing it slowly, on purpose. It has no place to build stress and work up internal chatter. That is because working slowly in today's world goes against every thought system. You can only work slowly if you do it deliberately. Being deliberate requires you to stay in the process, to work in the present moment.

After I finished the first instrument, I even went through the process of packing up my tools with meticulous care, just to walk ten feet away and unpack them slowly, one at a time, to start the second piano. Usually I would grab two handfuls of as much as I could carry and scurry through the orchestra chairs on stage trying to save time. Not this day, however. I was determined to carry out my goal plan of just trying to work slowly. We spend so much time rushing everything we do. Rushing had become so much of a habit that I was amazed at the amount of concentration it took to work slowly on purpose.

I took off my watch so I wouldn't be tempted to look at the time and let that influence my pace. I told myself, "I am doing this for me and for my health, both physical and mental. I have a cell phone and, if need be, I can call whomever and tell them I am running late, and that's the best I can do."

Into the second piano, I began to realize how wonderful I felt. No nervous stomach, no anticipation of getting through the day, and no tight muscles in my shoulders and neck, just this relaxed, peaceful, what-a-nice-day-it-is feeling. I would even go so far as to describe it as blissful. Anything you can do in a rushing state is surprisingly easy when you deliberately slow it down. The revelation for me came, however, when I finished the second piano. I very slowly put my tools away one by one with my attention to every detail. I continued my effort at slowing down as I walked to my truck in the parking garage a block away. I walked very slowly, paying attention to each step. This may sound nuts at first, but it was an experiment on my part. I was experiencing such an incredible feeling of peacefulness in a situation that usually had every muscle in my body tense that I wanted to see just how far I could intensify the situation with my effort.

When I got into the truck, the clock-radio came on with the turn of the key and I was dumbfounded. So little time had passed compared to what I had usually experienced for the same job in the past that I was sure the clock was incorrect. Keep in mind that I was repeating a process that I had done for many years. I have set up these pianos together sometimes five and six times a week. I had a very real concept of the time involved in the project. I pulled my watch out of my pocket as a second check. It agreed with the clock-radio that I had cut over forty percent off the time. I had tried to work as slowly as possible and I had been sure I was running an hour late. Yet I had either worked faster (which didn't seem possible, given my attention to slowness), or I had slowed time down (an interesting thought, but few would buy it). Either way, I was sufficiently motivated to press on with the experiment throughout the remainder of the day. I got so far ahead of schedule that I was afforded the luxury of a civilized meal in a nice restaurant, instead of the usual sandwich in the truck or no lunch at all.

I have repeated these results consistently every time I have worked at being slow and deliberate. I have used this technique with everything from cleaning up the dishes after dinner to monotonous areas of piano restoration work that I don't particularly enjoy. The only thing that foils the result is when I am particularly lacking in stamina and find myself drifting back and forth between working with slowness and succumbing to my feeling of, "I have to get this done quickly."

You can see how these four components are all part of the same thing. Each one needs and creates the other. When you work slowly, things become simpler. If you want to simplify something, break it down into small parts and work more slowly. Since all of these points take effort to develop and maintain, you will have greater success if you break down the time that you are going to apply on working at them into short intervals. You will find it much easier to stay with your effort if you do this.

For example, when I decided to work at slowness during that particularly long day, I didn't tell myself I was going to do it for the whole day even though I knew that was the goal. I would say to myself, "Let's just see if I can set my tool box down, open it and take my tools out slowly to prepare the first piano." When I had completed that, I would say, "Let's just see if I can tune the middle section of the piano slowly," and so forth. I simplified the whole process by breaking it down into small sections that would require me to focus for short periods of time. Working in this nature kept me succeeding at the task, and bit by bit brought the goal of maintaining that present-minded effort for the whole day towards me, without me reaching for it.

As you work at using these techniques, it will seem difficult at first. That is only because you have formed the habit of not working this way for so long, and our culture does not promote this way of going through the day. You are breaking away from everything you have been taught when you start down this path and begin to incorporate this perspective into your way of thinking.

Remember, you can apply these simple rules to any part of your life and to any activity you undertake. As you begin to evolve in this area, the Observer within you will become more and more apparent. You will start to watch yourself going through your daily life and become more and more aware of when you are living in the present moment and working in the process, and when you are not. This doesn't mean you will be able to control yourself all the time, though. That tempting mindset comes from slipping back into the "perfection" perspective that states, "Only when I can do this all the time will I have achieved my goal." Accepting that this is a lifetime effort, and that in the beginning your progress may seem almost unnoticeable, is part of the lesson to be learned. Keep thinking of the flower. Regardless of whatever stage of growth and evolution you are in, in every moment you are perfect at being who you are.

Non-judgment is the pathway to a quiet mind!

7

Equanimity and "DOC"

Equanimity is defined as calmness and even-temperedness. That would certainly seem like a quality necessary for happiness in life. Equanimity is a virtue worth every effort to develop. How do we work at equanimity? How do we bring this quality into our experience of life and how do we maintain it?

One of the signs that someone possesses this virtue is that they are undisturbed by the moment-to-moment ups and downs they experience in daily life. Things just don't seem to bother these people. Why is this? It is because equanimity comes from the art of non-judgment. Non-judgment quiets the internal dialogue of our mind.

We judge everything in life and most of it unconsciously. From the moment we wake up in the morning we start judging. We even judge what was happening when we were asleep: "I had a bad dream" or, "I slept great." We judge everything that comes toward us during the day. Every experience, every word that is spoken is evaluated and judged by filtering it through our opinions and our past experiences. This is necessary. It is how we make all of our decisions, whether they are of great importance or relatively insignificant. "I want this cereal for breakfast." This means that I have looked at all the available options for breakfast and made a judgment against everything I don't want this morning. Maybe tomorrow I will make a judgment against cereal in favor of eggs.

Judgment requires the process of evaluation, the process of comparison. This requires a point of relativity, an ideal. As I mentioned earlier in the book, judgments are always based on some preconceived idea of perfection. There is always an imagined ideal item, experience or circumstance that allows us and even compels us to pass judgment. We compare the present situation to either an imagined ideal situation of the same nature or to some past situation of the same nature. When you are unaware that it is happening, the problem with this process is that it is self-perpetuating and the "ideal" is always evolving. If you watch a movie and say, "That was a good movie," it means you are either comparing it to one or more movies you have seen in the past which were judged good or bad, or you are comparing it to some concept of what an ideal movie is. If you are comparing it to a movie you have seen in the past, ask yourself what made that particular movie good or bad...a judgment. Whether you judge the present movie as good or bad, the experience of watching it, evaluating it and finally judging it will go into your subconscious concept of the "ideal movie." This ideal concept evolves because your perceptions and priorities evolve throughout your lifetime. A good movie when you are thirty years old does not fit the same criteria of a good movie when you were seven.

Judgments are necessary to function in life, but they have a down side. The problem with the whole process of judging is that it is not executed with a detached nature. There is usually some emotion involved, and the amount of emotion is proportional to the perceived importance of the judgment. "The ideal breakfast this morning is Brand X cereal, but there is none so I will have eggs instead." This is not a particularly emotional judgment, but you do experience disappointment at some level. "Should I take this new job and move my family five states away from our friends?" is a different story. The emotions in this decision are much more pronounced because the outcome of the decision has such an impact on your life and the lives of your family. However, the emotions you experience have nothing to do with executing the decision. What is worse is that the emotions hinder you from thinking clearly, and give you the sense of struggle as you work at determining your best choice.

I have a private pilot's license. When you are working on your certificate, you are taught to fly the airplane based on procedures and to not allow emotions to enter into your decisions. At some point in the training, the flight instructor will pull the throttle all the way back to nothing, usually when you aren't expecting it, and say, "You just lost your engine, what are you going to do?" What you are going to do is the procedure you have been taught to do, one that you practice over and over so that it becomes a natural habit. One of my instructors told me that every time I got into the airplane, before I did anything else, she wanted me to run through the emergency "engine out" procedure. She instructed me to also make it the last thing I did before exiting the airplane. She said, that way, if the situation ever occurred in real life, there would be no emotion, no panic, and no extraneous dialogue stealing away precious seconds. I would just make decisions and execute them.

This works. The evidence of it can be seen in the heroic emergency landings made by commercial pilots and private pilots alike. I once heard a recording of a conversation that took place between a corporate pilot and air traffic control that was amazing. The pilot was in heavy fog with some critically needed instruments failing. He was flying at night in between mountains, and being told by the air traffic controller when to turn and what altitude and heading to hold. The pilot could see nothing out of the windows, and one wrong move would spell death in a fiery crash. Though his emotions were probably beating at his mind's door, screaming to be noticed, they had no power over him. He and his co-pilot were entrenched in practiced procedures, operating in total equanimity. They weren't judging their situation at all, just reacting to it. At that point in time, judging the circumstance would have brought mind-numbing emotions into the situation that could have meant the loss of their lives. The air traffic controller was just as process-oriented as the pilot and co-pilot. He knew that the pilots' lives depended on him operating clear of emotion. It was an incredible recorded conversation, and one that demonstrated that you are at your best when you are not operating under the influence of emotions and unconscious judgment-making.

The emotions attached to a judgment stem from a sense that "this is right and that is wrong" or "this is good and that is bad." Right and good make us happy while bad and wrong make us upset or sad. We feel that right and good are at least approaching "ideal," while wrong and bad are moving away from it. We all want to be happy and have an ideal life, but what constitutes right and wrong is neither universal nor constant. When Galileo was jailed 400 years ago for his observation that the earth was not the center of the universe, he was considered a heretic and speaking directly against God. Yet today we realize he was the only one back then who knew the truth. Instead of being wrong and bad he turned out to be right and good.

If you were to take a three-year-old child and follow him through his life, periodically asking him for his definition of ideal, you would get a different answer each time. At three he may just want a particular toy. At the age of ten he may want a new bike and no school, and at the age of nineteen, a college scholarship and a date with a particular person. By the time he reaches thirty, his idea of ideal might be a high-paying job, a family and a beautiful spouse. When he reaches fifty, he wants a new spouse and early retirement. At seventy he may want to either live fifteen more years or be ten again and back in school so he can fix all the mistakes he made and have an ideal life.

Our concepts of ideal and perfect are always changing. What we consider good or bad for ourselves doesn't stay the same. Of course, in regards to right or wrong here, we are not talking about eternal truths such as the idea that it is wrong or bad to take someone's life. What we are talking about are the evaluations and judgments we make unconsciously in every second of our lives that jump-start our emotions and bring us so much anxiety and stress.

Equanimity and "DOC"

What can we do about this unproductive habit? How can we escape this perpetual cycle? The first thing we need to do is to become aware of exactly when we are involved in the process of judging. Since this is all the time for most of us, we don't have to wait long for our first chance to observe ourselves participating in this exhausting act.

We must work at being more *objectively* aware of ourselves. We cannot refine any part of our daily thought processes if we are not separate from them. At first this seems to be a confusing concept to grasp, but with the slightest shift in perception it becomes clear. If you are aware of anything you are doing, that implies that there are two entities involved: one who is doing something and one who is aware or observing you do it. If you are talking to yourself, you probably think you are doing the talking. That seems reasonable enough, but who is listening to you talk to yourself? Who is aware that you are observing the process of an internal dialogue? Who is this second party that is aware that you are aware?

The answer is your true self. The one who is talking is your ego or personality. The one who is quietly aware is who you really are, the Observer. The more you become aligned to the quiet Observer, your true self, the less you judge. Your internal dialogue begins to shut down and you become more detached about the various external stimuli that come at you all day long. You begin to actually view your internal dialogue with an unbiased and sometimes amused perspective. I have had times where my ego is going on and on about something someone said to me that "it" considered "irritating," and I am very separate and unaffected. I feel as if I am invisible in a room watching someone complain about something that is completely unimportant to me. This also extends into experiences of personal stress such as job deadlines or finances. I have witnessed my ego rambling on about how I am not going to finish a job on time. When I am aligned to my true self, the Observer, I find myself aware of the stress that my ego is experiencing, but also unaffected by it. I have a sense of "that's just my ego fretting that it will experience disapproval by a certain party if it disappoints them by taking longer than it originally anticipated."

When you are aligned with your true self you are immune to other peoples' behaviors. When you feel that someone is acting inappropriately towards you, that comes from a judgment of the ego. From the perspective of the Observer, you find yourself just watching *their* ego rant and rave while you are listening quietly and unaffected.

The importance of knowing this is that when you decide to engage your practicing mind in any activity, you are evoking this alignment to the Observer, your true self. The *ego* is subjective. It judges everything, including itself, and it is never content with where it is, what it has, or what it has accomplished. The *Observer* is objective and there in the present moment. It does not judge anything as good or bad. It just sees the circumstance or action as "being." In other words, the circumstance "just is." Thus the Observer is always experiencing tranquility and equanimity.

Whether you are going for a job interview, trying to develop more patience with a difficult person or situation, or learning an art form, alignment with the Observer is tantamount to success and freedom from stress. This alignment assures an objective, no-expectations point of view. This contradicts the ego-driven mentality of "be the best," "nobody cares who came in second" and "I want it all."

Is there anybody out there who isn't tired of running as fast as they can to grab a mythical brass ring that we all know in our hearts doesn't exist? When a friend or family member falls short of something they considered an important goal, we console them with a detached wisdom that we don't apply to ourselves. Alignment to the Observer brings non-judgment and hence equanimity.

How do we become aligned to the *Observer*? How do we free ourselves from the confines of our ego? Though there are certainly a number of ways to accomplish this, in my opinion, the most effective method for creating this awareness spontaneously and effortlessly is meditation. Through meditation, it just happens on it's own over time. As you practice meditation, you become more and more aware of this silent observer within you. Through your effort, you realize that meditation is a process of quieting the mind and your attachment to the external world by going deep within yourself.

Meditation is not a religion. It has, however, been a part of virtually all major religions. Throughout time, all major religions have had a history of contemplative processes that deepen the individual's awareness of the God Force, or whatever you choose to call it. There is nothing scary about meditation, either. In fact, if you choose to pursue it, you will find it to be the part of your day that you look forward to the most because of the calming sense and clarity it brings into your life.

You can learn to meditate at any age and regardless of your physical condition. I have been meditating for over 27 years and I started out knowing next to nothing about it. In the beginning, I more or less felt my away along through my own chosen reading material and classes. Later, I studied in more structured environments and with more experienced people. The benefits of meditation cannot be described, they must be experienced, and I recommend it for everyone. There are many books and tapes available to get you started if you are interested. Mountain Sage Publishing has produced a very unique 2-CD meditation program titled *The Meditating Mind: Making Meditation a Part of Your Life,*, which can be used by both the complete beginner and also a more seasoned practitioner who is looking for a fresh approach. You can find out more about it in the back of this book.

With or without meditation, it is necessary to consciously work at shifting your alignment to the Observer. An effective adjunct method to meditation that I use for this purpose is what I call "DOC," which stands for Do, Observe, Correct. This technique can be applied to any activity in which you are trying to engage the practicing mind, but because it is easier to grasp when applied to a physical activity such as a sport, we will start with that.

I once read an interview with one of the Olympic coaches for the US archery team. He made the comment that the biggest problem he faced in coaching the American team was that they were so fixated on their score or the *result* of their shot. It was as if they were only drawing the bow and releasing the arrow to hit the bulls-eye and earn a good score. This was contrary to the Asian teams which, having grown up in a different culture, were consumed in the *process* of executing the proper technique that led up to releasing the shot. Where the arrow hit the target was almost unimportant compared to this motion of drawing the bow correctly and releasing the shot. They viewed the result with almost a detached indifference. For them, the desired goal was a natural result of prioritizing the proper technique of drawing the bow. They would do this without attachment to the result which hadn't happened yet. They operated in a completely different paradigm, and because of it, were very difficult to beat.

What I want you to get from this story is how the Asian archers are functioning in the DOC process. They draw the bow, they release the arrow, they observe the result and then they make corrections for the next shot. They DO, they OBSERVE, they CORRECT. There is no emotion in any of this. There are no judgments. It is simple and stress-free, and you can't argue with their technique because, for many years, they dominated the sport. However, go to any of our sporting events and nobody is having any fun unless they are winning. That is what we focus on. Our minds are reeling with judgments about where we are in the competition, and we are experiencing all the emotions that come with all that mental activity. The minds of the Asian archers were quiet and uncomplicated, and free from mental turmoil. The irony was that, when compared to the results-oriented Americans, the Asians were the ones who were winning. Now, our sports psychologists are teaching our athletes to think more along these lines.

This technique of DOC can and does happen in the background and very naturally at times. Give a basketball player ten shots from anywhere on the court. They will shoot at the target or DO, then they OBSERVE the shot unfold, and finally make CORRECTIONS based on what they observed. It happens in the background with no effort. What we want to do is make DOC a more natural way of how we approach life.

If, for example, you feel you are someone who tends to worry too much, then try to apply DOC to your actions. When you notice yourself fretting over something, you have accomplished the DO portion. OBSERVE this behavior that you want to change. In your observation of yourself worrying, you have separated yourself from the act of worry. Now realize that the emotions you are experiencing have no affect on the problem you are focusing on. Release yourself from the emotions as best as you can - that is the CORRECT portion - and try to look at the problem as an observer.

When you find yourself falling back into the fretting process, you start the cycle again. Just DO, OBSERVE, CORRECT, that's all there is, there is nothing else, no negative emotions or judgments. It's tiring at first. Remember, you are just breaking an unwanted habit of how you deal with problems. The old habit put all of your energy into fretting and very little of it into solving the problem. In a short time, the new habit of DOC will be a natural part of how you operate. You are just shooting arrows at a target: "Oops, missed that one to the left, that's all, shoot more to the right." It's a game of sorts and you are not letting the villain of emotions come into the game. Soon, the enjoyment that you experience from staying in the present moment makes hitting the darn target smack in the middle irrelevant. Don't confuse judging something with evaluating something. Evaluating comes before the action of passing judgment. You can't judge something if you haven't first evaluated it. You can make the decision to stop the process after evaluating and before it gets to a judgment. That is what you are doing in DOC. Your observation is the point where you are evaluating your process. Are you heading toward your goal? Then you jump immediately to CORRECT and skip the judgment because it has no value in your effort.

As you work at this technique, your ability to detach from the emotional content of a situation grows in strength. It becomes easier to apply this principle to more abstract circumstances such as personal encounters with difficult people or trying times. At first you must depend on your inner strength and determination to separate from a circumstance long enough to apply the principle of DOC. After that initial instant the game begins. I usually start by remembering a line from the first Star Wars movie when the Imperial fleet starts to fire on Luke, Lea and the gang. Faced with impossible odds, Han Solo says something like "This is when the fun starts." A line such as this is a great way to interrupt the momentum of your emotions when someone is being difficult with you, or you find yourself facing a personal challenge.

This really is when the fun begins because nothing is more satisfying than quieting the squawking voice of your frightened or insulted ego. In those moments, you realize that you really are separate from that angry or fearful voice and that you truly are the captain of your own ship and crew. In time, this process becomes easier. Like everything else you practice, you get better at it. As you practice, you become more aligned with the Observer within you and time begins to slow down with regard to these incidents. You see them coming toward you rather than finding them on top of you. Your reflexive movement *away* from the emotional reactions you are so accustomed to, becomes a habit and intuitive.

Once, I had booked a significant piano restoration project with a customer that fell through at the last moment. We had discussed the work several months ahead of time and worked out a time slot that would suit both of our schedules. My next move was to block out the several weeks of time that would be necessary for the job. This was about eight weeks into the future. Several days before I was supposed to pick up the work and begin the job, the customer notified me that he had changed his mind and wasn't going to do the work after all. People who are not self-employed are generally not acquainted with the situation of "when you're not working you are not earning money." This is particularly true in service-type businesses where you operate in piecework format. If you have five calls scheduled for the day and each one will bring in $50.00 dollars, your day's earnings start to dissolve very quickly if two of those calls aren't there. Even if the people apologize and reschedule, your weekly income has dropped and there is nothing you can do to affect that. In this situation which involved partial rebuilding work on a vintage grand piano, it was an extreme. It was Wednesday, and starting on the following Monday I had no work scheduled for the next two weeks. On top of that I was out several thousand dollars in income. It was not a good time. Immediately my ego kicked into high gear by turning on the anxiety machine and protesting the injustice of it all. This is when the fun begins.

The first thing I did was to step back and align with the Observer. Then I defined my "DOC" cycle for this particular instance. Because I had been working at this for some time, I hung up the phone with a deliberate, detached point of view. I expected the whole ego trip of anger and frustration to begin; I could actually see it coming before it was upon me. My cycle was this: When the anxiety would start I would observe and evaluate it. I realized that my ego's sense of the situation being unfair was just a judgment it was making out of fear of income loss. I also realized that the situation just "was as it was" and its value of being good or bad was merely an interpretation I could choose to accept or ignore. My correction was choosing to ignore my ego's sense of this being good or bad, fair or unfair. I told myself that the situation was merely the ebb and flow of financial energy into and through my life. Some jobs I would get, others I would not, and the jobs that I would get would have a value of satisfaction because they would be compared to jobs such as this one that I had not received. I focused on staying impartial and dealing with the situation in a detached manner despite how much the internal dialogue of my ego would be protesting: "But this is not fair, but this is wrong," etc. I looked at this as nothing more than a distraction. I would accept this situation as it *was,* not how my ego wanted it to be.

In this instance, the "DOC" cycle was comprised of my conscious participation in the whole process of seeing it coming, observing my internal dialogue with detachment and correcting my reaction to this dialogue. When I would complete the "DOC" cycle in this manner, the anxiety would subside and the internal dialogue would quiet down. In the beginning, it might return in fifteen minutes and perhaps I would start to indulge in the anxiety, but correcting this would be what I would prescribe for the next cycle. I did not judge my performance in this matter as good or bad. Keeping the impartial observer perspective is what I would work on as if I were watching a friend go through this and I was counseling them. Staying aware that I had a choice in how I would react to the feelings was what I strived for. Not falling victim to a conditioned response of my personality was my goal. I wanted to consciously make a habit of detaching myself and thereby use my privilege of conscious choice. The return periods of anxiety would steadily decrease in frequency and become less in intensity as I persevered at the "DOC" cycle. By the beginning of the next week they were all but gone. I considered this significant because there was a time in my life when this would have bothered me for weeks and the fretting would have really impacted the quality of my life.

In reality, this setback wasn't going to change my standard of living no matter how much my ego wanted to argue to the contrary. My true self knew that. The income would have been nice but I really didn't need it support my family. The whole situation was more of an inconvenience than anything else.

Equanimity and "DOC"

During the rest of the week I focused only on the solution to the problem. By Monday I had filled the two weeks with work and even had a little time left over to continue work on this book. In retrospect, the loss simplified my life at that time because it allowed me to balance the flow of an overburdened work schedule. The experience increased my knowledge of the value of what we are talking about here and how it truly does make life more of an adventure.

I have used this DOC method with every conceivable difficult situation. If somebody barks at me because they are having a bad day, my inner response is, "This is when the fun begins, let's go." As I said, though, I don't make my goal a perfect execution of staying detached and unaffected by other people's behavior or life's up and downs. That would be counter-productive because I would be substituting one kind of stress for another. I make my goal staying in the process of practicing DOC and being aware enough of internal dialogue to have a chance to use it.

You should also remember that when you start engaging your conscious "will" in how you handle difficult situations, you have to take it in short intervals, at least in the beginning. Otherwise you get too fatigued, and frustration is a danger. If you were to decide to take up jogging, you wouldn't go out and run a marathon on the first day. It takes time and practice sessions to build up the strength and endurance necessary to deal with the rigors of a race of that magnitude. Likewise, the stamina necessary for self-control is a process that you work at daily. You start with short intervals and allow yourself rest. If you are aware of when you are trying, then that means you are in the present moment and you have already won regardless of where you appear to be with regard to your personal goals. Your goals will always be moving away from you. That is the way we keep evolving.

Wisdom is not a by-product of age.
Teach and learn from
all those around you.

8

Teach and Learn From Children

If you have children, it is only natural to want to pass on to them what you have learned in your own life from both your struggles and your triumphs. We do this in an effort to save our children from having to repeat the same learning process we went through. The irony here, when we are talking about engaging the practicing mind, is that in some ways, children are ahead of adults in the way they process their lives. We have something to offer them but we also have something to learn from them.

What I have experienced when I am trying to pass on real knowledge to my own children is that it is not an easy task. The reason for this is that there is a large difference between children's and adults' perspectives about life. But I am not talking here about priorities, because I don't think we differ as much as we might think in that aspect. Kids basically want a sense of security, lots of free time and experiences that are fun and free from stress. Are adults any different in this regard? The differences I am talking about here are with regard to things such as a concept of time. When I was a child, I felt like the school day was an eternal event. Summer vacation seemed to go on for years. Time moved very slowly. If I tell my kids we are going someplace special next week, they whine about having to wait so long. Meanwhile, I am wishing that next week was a month away to give me more time to get everything done I need to before next week gets here. If I tell them to do their homework before they watch TV or get on the computer, they protest that the half an hour of homework will take forever.

As adults, we usually feel that life is going too fast. We feel there is too much to do in too little time, and most of us long for the simplicity of our school days when we were young. The older you get, the faster time seems to go. Seasons and years feel as if they are flying by. The time between when you were ten and twenty years old seemed like a century, and yet the time between say thirty and forty feels like two or three years. I am not really sure why this phenomenon occurs, but I have never met an adult who doesn't experience it. I think part of it is because when you are a child, hopefully you are still naive about much of the world's suffering that we perceive as adults. Life doesn't possess the quality of urgency it takes on in adult years.

Time perception is an integral part of the difference between adults and children. In general, children don't seem to have a sense of where they are going in life. There is today and that's it. They live in the present moment, but not really by their own choice; it's just how they are. There is the paradox here. What's frustrating as an adult, with regard to teaching them to stay in the present when they are engaged in something that requires perseverance, is that they can't see the point. Why work at something that requires a long-term commitment, a perception of time outside the present moment? All they know is what their perspective is as a child. They have no concept of what lies ahead. They don't see how discipline and effort pay such a great dividend over time as we do. This paradox is both their and our strengths and weaknesses in the same instant.

Look at an activity such as taking piano lessons. Children can't see the point in practicing because they have no concept of being able to play well and the enjoyment that would bring to them. That is why *they* get impatient. Why do it? Adults, however, do possess an understanding of the point of practicing, and it is for the exact opposite reason. They do have a concept of what it would be like to play well and that is the very reason *they* get impatient. They can't play well enough, soon enough. So as an adult, you have to notice that carefree nature that comes naturally to a child from living for and in the present. You have to try and help them to not "unlearn" that nature as they grow up in a world that constantly tries to push it out of them.

To me, the reason for working at all that I have been discussing in this book is obvious. It raises my level of control over my life and allows me to choose a path that is filled with more ups than downs. It makes me live in the present and brings happiness and peace in whatever I am doing in that ever-present moment. It makes me both aware that I am a conscious choice maker, and empowers me with privilege to make the choice.

I confess that teaching this to my daughters is a bit of a learning process that I am far from completing. What I have realized is that none of us learn anything except through our own direct experiences. Because of this, I try to teach in two ways. One is by reminding them of their past. They may not know where they are going, but they do know where they have been. I can take an event that was either a problem or a triumph in their lives and help them understand what qualities they brought into that event that made it so. This helps them to shift into an alignment with the Observer within themselves. They are more receptive to this when they are not distracted by the emotions that were present during the particular incident. I may do this when I am alone in the car with them and I know that their thought processes won't be interrupted by any outside events such as the TV or the telephone. I will start the conversation with something like, "Hey, remember last week when you got upset about what happened at school?" I may ask them how they feel about it now. This gives me a chance to make them aware of how their emotions affect their perceptions of events. By delaying the discussion of an incident for several days or a week after the fact, it gives them a chance to settle into a more detached perspective, and me a chance to decide how to best manage the discussion about that particular situation.

I remember an incident with my older daughter regarding a pogo stick. A while back, they had become popular again and my older daughter got one as a gift. She got really good on it in a short time and you couldn't get her off of the thing. Meanwhile, my younger daughter was given a gift certificate to a toy store for her birthday. When I took her to the store to use her certificate, she decided she wanted her own pogo stick. Well, by now the manufacturer's marketing departments had gotten involved and were making the pogo sticks look really cool with a lot of extra plastic fittings, but they were really just the same old pogo stick. When my younger daughter brought her new pogo stick home, you guessed it. The older daughter protested that hers was very plain and unexciting compared to the newer one that my younger daughter had bought. Even though they both gave the same experience when you were jumping up and down, my older daughter felt she was missing out. Here is how I resolved it in a way that I felt would make a lasting impression on her. I told my older daughter to give herself two weeks to get over her sense of having to have a new pogo stick like the one her sister had just bought. I told her, "You can swap with her at times if she wants and just keep jumping up and down for the next two weeks." I told her that it might seem hard to believe, but that the feelings she was experiencing right then were just emotions and that they would pass. I also told her, "If at the end of that time you still feel that you really have to have a pogo stick like hers, I will buy you one for executing the patience."

I knew this was another case of instant gratification, which never provides any lasting pleasure, and I wanted her to get past the emotion of the moment. About a week into the two-week period, they both had had more than enough jumping up and down on pogo sticks. Both pogo sticks were banished to the garage for retirement. After the allotted time, while riding in the car I reminded my daughter of our agreement and asked if she still wanted a new pogo stick. She thanked me and said,

"No, you were right, I don't really care about it anymore." I knew at some level that lesson would stay with her forever.

Another way of passing these concepts on to children is by teaching with your actions. Whether we are conscious of it or not, we are doing this to try to be aware of what we are putting out there. I remember a lot of things concerning adult behavior when I was growing up. Much of it was inappropriate behavior. We can't control the behavior of all the adults our children come in contact with during the day, but it is our behavior that has the most impact on them. A parent's behavior goes a long way toward manifesting a sense of what works and what doesn't in a child's mind. Actions definitely speak louder than words. When I have a difficult day with work, if I feel the experience will help my kids see how I coped with a situation, I will pass it on when I feel they are ripe for the knowledge. If I am under stress, I may let them know a little about it so they can see how I am dealing with it using my practicing mind. Your kids are always watching you. It is not necessarily a conscious observation, but it is one that is occurring nonetheless. I have seen both my best and worst qualities come out in my kids. Because of this I try to be aware of what I am silently teaching them and make it count.

Many adults make the mistake of thinking that because someone is younger than they are, they can't possibly learn something from them. This is both an egotistical and insecure point of view in my mind. It reminds me of my earlier comment of how we are so convinced that because we came along further in history, we must be more evolved than the people that lived in the distant past. I have met many young people, even children, who were more mature and better thinkers than some of the adults I know. Kids are dealing with a lot more today than most adults did as children. More is being pushed into their heads at an earlier age. For example, my daughters are doing types of math, such as algebra, several years earlier in their lives than I did when I was in school. Also, listening to children's points of view can be very enlightening because they tend to be more honest and open about how they feel.

My youngest daughter was involved in competitive gymnastics. As parents, we always came at these activities from the perspective that they should be the fun things in our kids' lives, not another stress factor. However, as my daughter progressed up through the competitive levels, the demands on her body and her time grew considerably. Three days a week she came home from school and had only about an hour to just sit. She would start on homework and have a snack. She then went to the gym until 9:00 p.m., which got her home about a half hour later. After eating a late dinner, at times she would work until almost 11:00 p.m. and then go to bed, to be awakened at 6:15 a.m. with only 45 minutes to get ready for school and start the cycle over again. All of this at the age of twelve years old. I felt it was really way too much, but initially she felt it was what she wanted. Several months into the school year though, she confided in me that she felt she never got time to just "sit still." She said, "All I do is rush from one thing to the next. I never have time to stop."

These moments offer such a perfect opportunity to both teach and learn from your children. Listen to what they are noticing about how they are living their lives. As you talk to them about real priorities, good perspective and engaging their practicing minds, it is a review lesson for yourself. Are you following the same advice you are giving to them? Are you teaching them that you have the same priorities for yourself? On more than one occasion when I have been over-worked, I have talked to my daughters about the importance of balance in life and how at times life needs to be re-adjusted to maintain that balance. Children have so much to offer because we can learn from them if we listen to ourselves as we are teaching them.

Teach and Learn From Children

With deliberate and repeated effort,
progress is inevitable.

Your Skills Are Growing

In every moment of your life your skills are growing. The question is, in which direction? What I have presented here in this book is not new knowledge by any means. It is centuries old and is constantly being relearned by new generations. When we understand how we work and stay in harmony with that knowledge, we feel a sense of control while we sit back and enjoy the experience of life flowing past us with ease. This knowledge commands us to stay in the present moment, which brings awareness to all that we do. This awareness gives us the opportunity to take control of the choices we make. It teaches us to stay focused on the process using the overall goal as a rudder to steer our course. When we make staying focused on the process our real goal, we experience a sense of success in every moment. Even when we feel we have fallen out of that focus on the process, the fact that we are aware of it means that we have come back into the present moment. It means that in this awareness, we have come so far at integrating these concepts into the way we live life. With this knowledge, we live each moment to its fullest and we experience it directly instead of indirectly. When we are in the present moment, we experience life as it happens and as it really is, rather than through the filters of anticipation, as in the future; or through analyses, as in the past. Most of us spend very little time in the present moment. We usually are either thinking about something that has not yet happened (and may never happen), or reliving something that already has. We waste the opportunity to experience what is real on something that is not.

We have discussed a number of techniques to help us develop these skills and to make the effort that is needed as little as possible. As you begin to use these techniques in different areas of your life, you will no doubt experience moments of frustration. This is, however, just the result of us holding imaginary ideals of how quickly we should master any new endeavor that we undertake. Again, we are taught this crippling mindset by almost every aspect of our culture, from the educational system with its grades, to the marketing media. Everyone wants to be number one, have the best, be an "A" student. This mindset can be unlearned though, and we must take on this challenge if we are to succeed at achieving any real happiness in life. Remember, this mindset is nothing more than a habit. We have habitualized the old way of thinking. Through our effort, we can make this new mindset into habit, which is much more conducive to a sense of overall well-being. We are making and reinforcing habits in every moment of our lives. Our reactions to people and circumstances are nothing more than habits. When we are aware of this through our practicing minds, we have the power to choose what traits we will manifest into our personalities. Now is the time to begin.

In closing I would like to say this. All cultures begin by expending all of their energy and resources into survival. If the culture survives this infancy, its people eventually pass the point of having to spend all of their time focused on staying alive. They get to a point of *what's* for dinner instead of *is* there dinner. Their days are filled with more and more free time. It is at this point that the society faces a fork in the road. We have been standing at this fork for quite some time. The one path states that you can spend at least a portion of this free time on expanding your spiritual awareness, your knowledge of your true self. The other path leads away from this truth into an endless cycle of meaningless self-indulgence which, at its core, is trying to fill the spiritual void that so many of us experience in our lives. The track record for all the great cultures that have come (and more importantly, gone) is unfortunately not a very good one. We can and must learn from this historical truth.

If you look at most of the things on which we place our daily priorities, you will notice that in times of personal crisis, they seem so insignificant. In those moments, the things that we usually pay so little attention to become everything to us. Our health and the health of our family and friends, who or what we feel the Creative Force is, become our sole priorities, and the dent in the car or the tight budget last month become such trivial concerns. Regardless of your religious belief, I would hope that you would feel that everything in life which you acquire of a spiritual nature will be with you forever. Everything else will not. Houses, jobs, and cars come and go; you, however, are eternal.

With this in mind, take time regularly to review all the things that you have acquired in your life all the way back to your childhood. What you will notice is that the toy that was everything to you when you were a child has no significance to you at all now, and yet at the time, getting it consumed your thoughts. What you may also notice is that the joy in the memory of that toy is not in the toy itself, but in the simplicity of life back then, a simplicity that was rooted in your unknowing, present moment living. If you look at all the "things" that you had to have in your life through the years, you begin to see that you don't really care about most of them anymore, certainly not the material ones. Things like the car or the furniture lose their importance and value to you over time. You may even wonder what you saw in many of those things in the first place.

That moment of realization is a good time to notice if you are just repeating that process of struggling to acquire things that you are convinced will end the anguish and twinges of emptiness you feel inside. You come into this world with only your true self, and you leave the same. Everything that you acquire spiritually expands your true self and becomes part of you forever. We need to get off of this self-destructive train that runs on the tracks of instant gratification. All things of lasting and deep value require time and nurturing and come to us only through our own effort. I think everybody out there is aware of this at some level. We just get distracted by information to the contrary that comes at us every day. You can eliminate a certain amount of that by paying attention to what you expose yourself to in the way of media, be it TV, music or reading material. If it doesn't enrich you, then you don't need it.

Most importantly, if we make our first item of business to develop our practicing mind, then the process of *becoming* is an adventure, and we are filled with peace instead of struggle. I have put down here for you what I am learning in my own life through my own efforts. I hope that it helps you in the same way that those before me have helped me, by taking the time to put down what they have learned. Remember, none of this is new. They are just the eternal truths that we have learned and re-learned over the centuries from those who have questioned and found peace in the answers. This is when the fun begins.

More Products to Quiet the Mind from Thomas M. Sterner

- ॐ *The Practicing Mind: Bringing Discipline and Focus Into Your Life* (4-CD Audio book, unabridged)

- ॐ *The Meditating Mind: Making Meditation a Part of Your Life* (2-CD Audio Set)

- ॐ *The Total Mindset: The Practicing Mind* (Paperback)/*The Meditating Mind* (2-CD Audio Set)

- ॐ *The Total Mindset: The Practicing Mind* (Audio book)/*The Meditating Mind* (2-CD Audio Set)

Available from Mountain Sage Publishing
www.thepracticingmind.com

Mountain Sage Publishing
products to quiet the mind